When Life Shows Up

When Life Shows Up

*A Spiritual Disciplines
Development Devotional*

Rev. Dr. Charles B. Mayson

and

Victoria Mastrovito

Library of Congress Control Number: 2020923019

HARDBACK: 978-1-953791-62-7
PAPERBACK: 978-1-953791-61-0
EBOOK: 978-1-953791-63-4

Ordering Information:

For orders and inquiries, please contact:
1-888-404-1388
www.goldtouchpress.com
book.orders@goldtouchpress.com

Printed in the United States of America

Introduction

In 2010 I published a book titled *When Life Shows Up*. The gist of the book was that as Christians we are not immune from the struggles of this world. In fact, in God's Word He tells us we are to expect the lost world to rise up against us. Knowing that, it is best to be prepared and how better than to develop and practice spiritual disciplines.

So the book talks about seven spiritual disciplines. These disciplines can be practiced anywhere by anyone without any special equipment. No deep theological understanding is needed.

This devotional is a companion volume to that earlier book. You do not have to read the book to get full meaning and value from this devotional. It is certainly a standalone volume.

My sister is the co-author of this devotional – neat, right? We alternated writing each week of the fifty-two week project. I'm excited about how our work reads so differently yet gives the same message – God's input obviously!

So the devotional works like this. Each day you will be exposed to a spiritual discipline. At the end of the week you will have covered seven spiritual disciplines. At the end of the year you will have been exposed to each of the disciplines fifty-two times.

It is our prayer that after this devotional period you will have formed some great habits as it relates to these seven disciplines, incorporating them into your daily lives seamlessly and productively.

Lastly, at the end of each daily reading there is some room for **Reflection**. Some days have lots of room, some not so much. Part of the discipline process is to Reflect, even briefly, about what comes to mind after each daily reading. This practice will help firm up for God's future use, in your life, the thoughts for each day.

Hold on for a wonderful journey this year as God has led Victoria and me to be your tour guide through His Word for the purpose of developing solid spiritual disciplines.

God bless and Amen!

Acknowledgement

I need to take a second to thank most emphatically my friend Sara and her sister Jeanne (pronounced Zhahn) for editing this project. A 364 day devotional has a lot of words. Words make sentences and paragraphs that even with correction prompts from Microsoft Word, have to be checked. I am a terrible editor of my own work or anyone else's for that matter. So it is with great admiration and humility that I thank my friends and applaud their unique skill set. God bless you both.

Worship

Genesis 1:1
"In the beginning God created the heavens and the earth."

Week One   **Day One**

"…God created…"!! God created! This simple phrase is full of wonder and awe. God created the earth and the sky. God created the animals, the birds, the breeze blowing through the trees. God created me! What else can I do but worship the Creator? What else can I do but sing God's praises? When we gather together and see the wonder of God's creation in the others around us, I can do no less than sing for joy. Praise God. Praise God. Praise God.

Reflections

Bible Reading

Psalms 119:160a
"The sum of Your Word is truth…"

Week One   **Day Two**

In a world where the truth is hard to find and more often than not spun to articulate the message or agenda of the speaker, what are we to do? On the other hand, we are led to believe that those with money, prestige, fame and influence have a market on the truth because they happen to have a platform to speak on. What are we to believe? Whose words are we to take for truth?

God's Word is what we take for truth. A daily dose of His Word will enable us to sort through, correctly, the clutter we are confronted with each day. The Psalmist wrote, "the sum of Thy Word is truth," and he was exactly right. God's Word is truth and will never be anything less. The world and its media has an agenda, whatever that may be, but God has only the desire to have us accept and follow Him.

Reflections

Prayer

1 Thessalonians 5:17
"… pray without ceasing..."

Week One   **Day Three**

There was a pilgrim who decided to repeat a certain prayer thousands of times a day as he walked the countryside. He tells how at some point in his repetition, the prayer became like breathing and he could not stop. He no longer had to make a decision every day; it was part of his nature, as automatic as breathing. This is where we start. A daily conscious decision to pray will bring us into deeper relationship with God and soon we can do nothing less.

"They" say that it takes about 30 days to form a habit. Commit yourself to 30 days of deliberate prayer with God. All throughout your day, stop and praise Him or thank Him or ask for forgiveness or just chat with Him. Set an alarm; decide that every time you get a cup of coffee or go to the bathroom (or refrigerator or for a walk) you pray. It really doesn't matter-spend as much time as you can with God. Before you know it, it will become apart of your nature, as automatic as breathing. And your relationship with the Father will deepen.

Reflections

Meditation

Psalms 19:14
"Let the words of my mouth and the meditation of my heart
be acceptable in Your sight,
O Lord, my Rock and my Redeemer."

Week One   **Day Four**

I need God to guide me in meditation. My mind is so busy, flitting from one thought to another. Left to my own devices I will follow each thought as it enters my mind. My thoughts are distractions in meditation, so I humbly ask God to guide me as I ponder His Word. I don't have to latch on to each stray thought. Instead I can rest in the assurance that God is guiding my meditation and return my thoughts to Him. I may have to do this many times, but each time I do I know that God is smiling at me as I return to Him.

Reflections

Physical Wellness

Matthew 3:10b
"…therefore every tree that does not bear good fruit is cut
down and thrown into the fire."

Week One   **Day Five**

Spiritual, physical and mental fitness needs to be a balanced
effort as we grow. As kids we were always encouraged to
develop physically by getting involved with activities at school
and in the neighborhood. We were led to give our best in
school so mentally we would develop. And if you were like me
you were dragged to church to build a spiritual foundation.

Matthew, in his Gospel, wants us to know that it is
important that our 'whole being' be recognized as people of
God. In Matthew 3:10, he tells us that "therefore, every tree
that does not bear good fruit is cut down and thrown into the
fire." If our overall physical wellness is not providing fruit, then
we are not exhibiting the character traits necessary to influence
those around us. This is so important that Matthew says if we
call ourselves Christians and are not setting an overall holistic
example, we are out of God's will and need to be redirected.

Reflections

Fellowship

Galatians 2:9
"And recognizing the grace that had been given to me, James and Cephas and John, who were reputed to be pillars, gave to me and Barnabas the right hand of fellowship, so that we *might go* to the Gentiles and they to the circumcised."

Week One   **Day Six**

Fellowship is particularly hard for me since I tend to isolate and avoid people in general. But I also understand and have realized the benefits of fellowship. One of the many facets of fellowship that I particularly appreciated is accountability. Christian fellowship is, in part, allowing others to hold you accountable. I want the people in my life that I trust and respect to call me on my stuff. If I'm behaving in a way that would cause someone else to sin or in a way not pleasing to God, I need my peeps to say, "Hey, what's up with that?"

In todays scripture, Peter, apparently, has been treating the Gentile Christians differently than the Jewish Christians when other people are around. Paul calls Peter on his stuff. He lets Peter know that he was being inconsistent with the two groups. This is a perfect example of how Christian fellowship is about accountability.

Reflections

Service

Isaiah 32:17
"And the work of righteousness will be peace,
and the service of righteousness,
quietness and confidence forever."

Week One   **Day Seven**

One of the most important lessons the Holy Spirit has taught me come from service work. I have learned that opportunities to serve others – for and through Christ – has little to do with the other people involved. It's all about me?? Service opportunities are simply tools and methods God uses to further His cause and draw me closer to Him. Sure, the people on the receiving end of my work benefit but answering the call of service is all about me and my relationship with God and how He uses me to further His will.

And God certainly gives us freewill to turn down the opportunities. The Bible is full of examples of people who have declined an assignment from God. It is never pretty for the refuser. However, the task always gets done – God always, always, always finds someone who "love their neighbor as themselves" (Matt 22:39). God always, always, always finds someone who is obedient.

Reflections

Worship

Psalms 2:11
"Worship the Lord with reverence."

Week Two   **Day One**

If we want to move forward as Christians there is only one way to do so and that is to worship God. He created us to worship Him and that is what we must do. David, in this Psalm, cautions us to worship with reverence. We wonder why our spiritual journey gets bogged down; it may be that we are not approaching God in the correct posture.

He is worthy of our praise. If we approach Him like He is a genie we want wishes from or Santa Claus we give our list of wants to, then we are wrong. He is not a kindly old Granddad we can just approach as we see fit. We must approach Him regularly, with humility and the knowledge of our brokenness.

The good news is that if we approach God like David instructs, look at Psalms 2: 12, "…How blessed are all who take refuge in Him"! God does not expect us to be perfect, He just wants us to see Him for who He is.

Reflections

Bible Reading

Revelation 19:13
"He is clothed with a robe dipped in blood;
and His name is called The Word of God."

Week Two   **Day Two**

As Protestant Christians we believe that Jesus will return and reign on earth for one thousand years before He closes out human history. The Book of Revelation tells of His return and His coming as a conqueror this time, not as a servant like before. This event has been foretold throughout the Bible and for believers it is no surprise.

The disciple John writes in the Book of Revelation that when Jesus returns, "He is clothed with a robe dipped in blood; and His name is called The Word of God." So, aligned with God and His Word, Jesus is considered the truth that has been prophesied for all time. Jesus' actions from the beginning of time reflect the truth that God has established in His Word. Jesus' presence in the close of human history therefore can be counted as truth! God's Word, the Bible, is the truth He has given us so we can know for sure how to interact with Him.

God does not want His requirements for us to be a mystery. He wants us to know exactly what His purpose for our life is. He has provided a manual of sorts for that purpose. Our problem is that we do not like reading the instructions, we just want to start putting the project together on our own. I'm just saying!

Reflections

Prayer

Luke 11:1
"And it came about that while He was praying in a certain
place…one of His disciples said to Him,
Lord teach us to pray…"

Week Two   **Day Three**

One of the greatest examples for our need to pray is that Jesus
did so. Jesus, throughout His ministry, was always taking time
to pray. In fact, He used a lot of common sense in His timing.
He knew the day would be busy so He got up early in the
morning and got it done.

As a Pastor I took heed to Jesus' timing. As soon as it
was sociably appropriate to start calling, my phone would
begin to ring. I knew this would happen and so I rose early
in the morning, exercised and did my daily Bible reading and
devotional work.

In my book, the chapter on prayer was one that really
stretched me. I am not poetic or a guy who can pray with ease. I
had to learn to discipline myself to practice this important way
of communicating with God. We need not pray for answers,
we just need to pray to make contact, says Oswald Chambers.

Reflections

Meditation

Deuteronomy 6:6
"And these words, which I command you today,
shall be on your heart"

Week Two   **Day Four**

The Jews practiced this commandment later by wearing phylacteries. These were small boxes or bags with the Shema scripture in it. They would fasten it to their foreheads. They do this as a way of keeping God's Word close to them.

It is largely symbolic and reminds them of how important God's Word is. We read it in our daily devotional time, set it down and go about our day. At times we recall our lessons from our devotional time, but life gets busy. I am so guilty of engaging God in prayer, then letting my day keep me from seeing His application of our talk.

I always try to write a little something after each devotional reading to try to reflect, even if briefly, on what I just read. It is now in my mind and God can bring it back to my memory when I need it. Like a primed pump, the information is there and God draws it out at the correct time. He can use a dry pump and will but He wants us to do what we can to be ready. Prime the pump, folks!

Reflections

Physical Wellness

Genesis 6:3
"The Lord said My Spirit shall not strive with man forever,
because he also is flesh…"

Week Two   **Day Five**

God created us as perfect human specimens and we were
designed to live forever. Adam and Eve messed that up, sin
entered the world and our human forms now would die.
Nevertheless, God still loves us and even in this passage was
giving Noah time to build an Ark to save his family and two
of every kind of animal.

Because we are in a constant state of decay it is important
to work to maintain ourselves physically because God has a
job for us to do. We cannot be part of His solution if we are
broken down. We cannot be helpful to others if we do not
practice self-care.

God's Spirit abides in us, it is an honor to be His host.
Would we invite company into our messy house or workspace?
Why would we allow our Holy God to reside in anything less
than the best we can provide? God is not looking for glamorous
lodgings, He just wants us to be creating an environment He
can work with. He can make the stones get up and talk or a
donkey for that matter, yet He expects us to be responsible for
our "house."

Reflections

Fellowship

Philippians 3:10
"That I may know Him and the power of
His resurrection and the fellowship of His suffering,
becoming conformed to His death."

Week Two   **Day Six**

Paul is talking about the prize of the Christian life. In this life we were never designed to go it alone. As we develop this discipline, we will see that we will share with other Christians the ups and downs of life. Paul says here we will "be conformed to His death." We may not all be crucified like Jesus but we will certainly pass from this life to the life He offers in heaven.

In a Twelve Step program I am involved in, we say "a problem shared is a problem halved." God wants us to walk with others during this journey on earth. He knows by ourselves we will burn out and die, much like a hot coal separated from the rest of the fire.

This is not easy for some of us overachievers but it is a discipline we can get better at. We are herd animals not meant to be alone. We need others to help hold us accountable. We need others to help hold us up at times. Mostly we need others to share the joy of Christian fellowship with. The world is not going to participate with us in that.

Reflections

Service

Ruth 1:16
"Ruth said, do not urge me to leave you
or turn back from following you…"

Week Two   **Day Seven**

One of my most favorite books of the Bible is the Book of Ruth. This lady is a Moabite woman who thought so much of her Jewish mother-in-law she decided to dedicate her life to serving her. What? In this passage Naomi, Ruth's mother-in-law, has urged Ruth to go back to her own people, marry and have a family.

When we allow God to lead us in our daily walk with Him, He is going to want us to do for others. He spreads His blessing this way. He gives to some, who are to distribute to the rest of His people. It seems inefficient but it's the way He chose to disseminate His Word and blessings. He said the poor will always be with us. Why? Because He wants us to serve them with the blessings He has given us.

Ruth's life was a struggle for a while but because of her desire to serve she was included in the lineage of King David and then Jesus. A foreign woman was blessed to serve and then be part of the greatest birth in history.

Reflections

Worship

Psalms 2:11b
"Worship the Lord with reverence…"

Week Three   **Day One**

In some passages of the Bible glory is translated as PRESENCE. We are always in God's presence. Coming to believe that this is true may take a while, but when we do, we can receive great calm and joy, and be moved to the need to call out in thanksgiving to God for God!

Psalms 139 says "whither can I go from Thy presence?" The answer is-nowhere! Wherever I go, whatever I am doing, God is there with me. Again Psalms 139, "such knowledge is too wonderful for me." Our response to this knowledge of the constant presence of God is to worship God, giving thanks for God's Presence, Light and Love.

Reflections

Bible Reading

Genesis 1:3
"God said, 'Let there be...'"

Week Three   **Day Two**

Today the beliefs about how the world came into being are numerous. There are so called experts that would like for us to believe that our wonderfully balanced planet came forth from an accident. Others would like for us to believe that some cosmic collision of matter formed over millions of years the world we live in. I could go on but just because these folks talk loud and often does not mean it is the truth, it just means they can talk loud and often.

Moses wrote in the Book of Genesis that "in the beginning God," was the source of all creation. He goes on to add details of how the world we live in was formed. He details that "God said, let there be light; and there was light." The truth the Bible indicates is the one we need to hold on to. It is the correct revelation of our worlds beginning and is the only explanation that answers all the questions humanity has had over time. Truth is truth and the Bible is the source of truth for us.

Reflections

Prayer

Philippians 4:6
"Do not be anxious about anything, but in everything,
by prayer and petition, with thanksgiving,
present your requests to God."

Week Three   **Day Three**

This little verse is a format we can use to help us be in the right frame of mind when we feel the need to ask God for something. This type of prayer is known as supplication.

First, we come to the realization that God is God! This may sound silly, but we need to realize that we are not God. We don't have to make the sun come up or set. We don't have to figure out what is right for us and for everyone in our lives. We need to come to a place in our thinking that God has theirs covered. God is God, we are not! This can be a real relief for us, and then we are moved to give thanks to God, for God. After giving thanks we are in the correct position to ask God for what we want or need, always ending the prayer with 'Thy will be done.' This is not an easy way to pray, but it is the humble way to pray. Try it.

Reflections

Meditation

Genesis 24:63
"Isaac went out to meditate in the field toward the
evening…"

Week Three   **Day Four**

Isaac realized that in order to mediate he had to get away from EVERYTHING that was going on in his household. He knew that he would only be distracted by what was going on around him. So, he set a time and place to meditate. That's how important meditation is. We need to make an appointment with ourselves – one that we will honor – to practice this spiritual discipline.

Meditation isn't always easy, at first. It takes practice. Find a time during the day where you can go off by yourself and carve out some time. Start with 10 – 15 minutes at first; then, gradually increase that time as necessary. Make it clear to all those potential disturbances that this is your time – no interruptions. Period. Make this important.

Reflections

Physical Wellness

Mark 2:3
"And they came bringing to Him a paralytic,
carried by four men…"

Week Three   **Day Five**

One of the myths that the evil one wants us to believe is that God does not care for us. He is busy pleasing Himself, chasing His own agenda. Our well-being physically, mentally and spiritually is part of the total readiness God wants for us. There is no part of our well-being that is more or less important to Him who created us.

In Mark's Gospel we find Jesus doing amazing things in the lives of believers. In Mark 2:3, four friends of a paralytic brought him before Jesus. In fact they were so persistent they lowered him down from a hole they made in the roof! Jesus responded to their faith and showed His concern for man's overall health by healing the paralytic. It is God's desire to heal all portions of our well-being.

Reflections

Fellowship

Romans 8:16, 17a
"The spirit Himself bears witness with our spirit that we are
children of God…fellow heirs with Christ."

Week Three   **Day Six**

We aren't in this alone. Fortunately, there are a ton of us
Christians running around - everywhere. We are all – equally -
children of God. And just as a parent loves nothing more than
seeing their children playing and interacting lovingly, I can
only imagine God wants the same for His children. Hence
fellowship. There are countless benefits of being with other
Christians, but most importantly, God expects us to come
together, support one another, and fellowship!

Reflections

Service

Exodus 3:10
"Therefore, come now, and I will send you…
so that you may bring My people…out…"

Week Three   **Day Seven**

Service is an honor. It is an honor because it is an assignment God would like, specifically, for you to do. The Bible is full of examples of people God handpicked for a particular task: Moses and Aaron were chosen to lead the Israelites out of Egypt; Bezalel and Oholiab were tasked as the chief craftsmen for the tabernacle; Mary became the virgin mother of Jesus; and, of course, the ultimate – God asked Jesus to die for all of our sins.

And, yes, you can refuse the assignment. You can question your ability to do the service work. You can beg God to choose an alternative. Moses offered God five excuses as to why he wasn't the best choice to lead his people to the Promised Land. The Virgin Mary certainly had questions for God. Even Jesus asked God to "take this cup from me". Ultimately, when God leads us to service work, He will equip us and guide us so that we may, indeed, be successful and faithfully carry out His will.

Reflections

Worship

Mathew 2:2
"For we saw His star in the east,
and have come to worship Him"

Week Four   **Day One**

It is now possible with modern technology to map the positions of the stars and planets on any given date in history. Using math, that is actually old math from the 1400's, astrologers can accurately determine what star the Wisemen from the east were looking at that led them to Bethlehem. God is good and it's just another verification that science proves the Biblical account of Jesus' birth.

These men of science came not out of basic curiosity about the signs they had seen in the heavens but to worship the infant child they found foretold lying in a manger wrapped in cloths. After lots of miles, demanding some serious logistical support they came to worship God in His human form.

What are we willing to do to give thanks and honor to the Creator of the heavens and the earth? What are we willing to sacrifice to thank God for creating us? We will go to great lengths to satisfy our own wants and desires. There is no obstacle too great to keep us from our own interest. We need to let nothing stand in our way of giving praise and honor to our Creator.

Reflections

Bible Reading

Exodus 3:13
"And God said to Moses, I Am who I Am…"

Humans are the same today as they have been throughout history. Folks talk of the "good-ole-days"; actually, all the days have been the same. Yes, there have been advances in technology, medicine, inventions of all types but people have not changed. The environment, government and economy might change but people will always be people.

God's chosen people were in captivity in Egypt and wanted to be freed. The Bible tells us that God selected a man named Moses to lead His people to freedom. Moses was not as confident with the plan as God was and began to ask questions, one of which we find in the Book of Exodus. Moses asks God, "The God of your fathers has sent me to you. Now they may say to me, what is His name?" God tells Moses to call Him "I Am Who I Am." The God of the Bible is and has always been and remains the same for us "yesterday, today and tomorrow." (Hebrews 13:8) The Bible is clear that we follow a constant, unchangeable God. Amen!

Reflections

Prayer

Deuteronomy 4:7
"For what great nation is there that has a god so near to it as is the Lord our God whenever we call on Him?"

Week Four   **Day Three**

It is easy for me to forget all that God has done for me. I get busy with my day and then before I know it, I have not given God any credit for my blessed life. I know maybe I am the only one who does that but bottom line, it makes me ungrateful. That is not the posture I want before God.

In this passage, Moses is attempting to rally the troops. He is speaking to the generation of Israelites who will soon enter the Promised Land. He wants them to remember how great their God is. These folks were not part of the great exodus from Egypt, the Red Sea crossing or even the beginning of the flow of mana.

What a great question: is there any other nation they have encountered on their journey that has a god as responsive as our God? Of course, all other gods are false. We are in a unique position to have the one true God. We can call on Him at any time through our prayers. We can gain access to Him without any intermediary or having to be in a special building or body position.

Reflections

Meditation

Luke 2:19
"Mary treasured up all these things pondering in her heart"

Week Four   **Day Four**

When I was in high school my Dad was always telling me to "stop and smell the roses." Of course, I had no clue what he was trying to tell me and I was a teenager who knew everything, so I dismissed his advice. Wrong move, Charlie.

As I started on my real spiritual journey through seminary and became a Pastor these words often came back to me. Now I am older and they really are a significant part of my daily spiritual routine. I am taking time to listen for God's good orderly direction. I am taking time to be grateful for His blessings.

Mary had just given birth to Jesus and had been visited by a bunch of shepherds. They had told her some wonderful things about her baby. She knew He was special, so some of the information was just verification of what she knew. Some, however, was brand new news. How important for this young teenager to do a better job than I did when given so much to think about.

Reflections

Physical Wellness

Acts 9: 8-9
"Though his eyes were open he (Saul) could see nothing...
three days without sight."

Week Four   **Day Five**

There is nothing more miserable than losing a function of your body. Broken leg, torn shoulder muscle, bad back, I could go on. How limited do you feel when all your parts do not function as designed by God? I have been blessed to have good health all my life and had very limited times when my parts acted up.

I think about Paul in this passage as he had to struggle without his sight. He did not know it would be just three days nor did he know what would become of him if this ailment continued for a lifetime. This was not an ordinary human condition; this was an act of God.

Every time I read this passage, I am reminded of how important it is for me to take care of the resources God has provided for me. I do not know what will happen in the future with my health. I do know how to best maintain that valuable resource in the meantime. We cannot serve God if we have not maintained the vessel He gave us to serve with. We do not know what may happen, like Paul's issue. We can, however, work with what we do know. Staying health is not a mystery, it is a choice.

Reflections

Fellowship

Psalms 55:14
"We who had sweet fellowship together,
walked in the house of God"

Week Four   **Day Six**

Has anybody ever played golf by themselves? I have on occasion. In my case, the very rare time I make a good shot, I look around and there is no one to share the miracle with. I do enjoy the solitude and the opportunity to reflect on whatever is going on in my life, but I hate missing the opportunity to share a good event.

As a Pastor I often heard someone say there is no need to fellowship with others. I am a loner, I do alright by myself. So often we allow alright to be our goal when God wants the best for us. Yes, at times we do not have fellowship opportunities, but mostly we do, therefore, it is a choice.

In this verse David has written a song that helps him sort through a tough time. Part of the healing he receives is due to the fellowship of his other believers. David understands the value of solitude but he also understands the need for fellowship. There is a strength and power in the group.

Reflections

Service

Ephesians 4:12
"For the equipping of the saints for the work of service…"

Week Four   **Day Seven**

There is nothing more maddening than being asked to do a job and not having the resources to do it. As an army officer, one of my primary concerns was providing my troops with what they needed to do the job asked of them. I was astounded by some of my peers who did not see that as a major concern. What?

Paul in this letter is speaking on the subject of spiritual gifts. He was letting these new Christians know how important it was to use them to serve their fellow man. So often we see folks using their God given gifts for their own benefit, lifting themselves up with these assets with no regard to the real purpose for them.

We are all commanded to serve in God's plan for us. He has provided us all with certain resources to accomplish His goals for us. If we are feeling like we are not moving forward in our spiritual journey one of the first things to check is how we are using the gifts God has given us.

Reflections

Worship

John 4:22
"We worship that which we know…"

Week Five Day One

As we saw yesterday, daily Bible reading allows us to get to know God. In fact, all seven spiritual disciplines are avenues in getting to know Him. Dr. Mayson writes in his book, *When Life Shows Up*, "Worship is a must to know the heart and mind of God. It gets you in the correct posture before Him so that you can develop and grow in your understanding, your faith, and your obedience" (pg. 89). Further, Mayson states, "Worship implies a group activity, a collective joining of hearts, souls, and minds for a common purpose" (pg. 89). We must know God (Bible Reading) to worship Him and in worshipping Him, we get a deeper knowledge of Him.

Reflections

Bible Reading

Matthew 1:20a
"An angel of the Lord appeared to him in a dream, saying…"

Week Five   **Day Two**

The Bible is our 'user's manual'. God gives us instructions and guidance through His Word. God uses the Bible to reveal His nature and today's verse shows us that the Lord uses many different avenues and tools to communicate with us. However, there is a catch: we must actually *read* what the Bible says.

This is why daily Bible reading is so crucial for our growth and relationship with God. If we aren't listening, we don't know what God is saying, what God intends for us, or even how God communicates with us. Some will argue that the Bible is just a bunch of fables with morals attached. If you read consistently enough, I promise that you will begin to hear God's voice directed at you! So many times in reading my daily Scriptures has God specifically answered a prayer, shown me direction, or simply let me really know He is there!

Reflections

Prayer

2 Chronicles 7:12
"Then the Lord appeared…and said…
I have heard your prayer…"

Week Five   **Day Three**

God does, indeed, hear our prayers. This is demonstrated and chronicled over and over again in the Scriptures. 1 John 5:14 assures us that we can be *confident* that He hear us and 1 Peter 3:12 says that the Lord is *attentive* to our prayers. In a day and age where communication between humans is faltering, isn't it relieving and reassuring to know that *someone* is listening to everything that comes from your heart?

Reflections

Meditation

Matthew 6:21
"Where your treasure is, there will your heart be also."

Week Five   **Day Four**

Wow! Isn't this true?! Think about it: if you're consumed with, say, money (or alcohol or knickknacks, for example), that's all you think about. We spend our time obsessing and planning for things that govern our heart; oftentimes to the exclusion of those around us.

What would happen, though, if our hearts were centered on God? If He were the treasure that we focused on? Our whole lives would change, for the better! We would be kinder and more giving and happier, I think. And what better place to live, than in the presence of God?

Reflections

Physical Wellness

1 Corinthians 6:19
"Or do you not know that your body is a temple of the Holy
Spirit within you, whom you have from God?"

Week Five   **Day Five**

A Christian's body is home to the Holy Spirit. We keep
hammering this, don't we? Of all the spiritual disciplines
Charlie has identified, this one "dogs" me the most. Although
I'm wicked active, I'm not a big fan of exercise, eating right
(or at all, for that matter!), and not putting toxins into my
body. There, I said it. But as I've been working on this project,
this whole "Christians' bodies are temples" thing - and the
importance of keeping that temple holy – has been making a
big impact on me.

So, believe me, I'm struggling right there with those of you
in my boat. Let's support one another through this and try to
really understand and comprehend how truly important this is.

Reflections

Fellowship

Genesis 2:18
"Then the Lord God said,
'It is not good for man to be alone...'"

Week Five   **Day Six**

God made us in His image, which includes His preference for relationships. God is a relational entity. Therefore, we inherently have the need to be with others. Of course, in this particular Scripture, God was specifically talking about Adam needing a partner, but from the very beginning of time, God has recognized the benefits and the vital need we have for fellowship.

But it goes deeper: we are encouraged to fellowship with like-minded people, people who also love the Lord and subscribe to His way of thinking and living. Fellowship allows us to interact with others in a deep, meaningful way that can impact and enhance our lives. Fellowship also allows us (and others) to develop our relationship with God.

Reflections

Service

Titus 3:8b
"...so that those who believe God may be careful to engage in good deeds."

Week Five　　　　　　　　　　　　　　　　　　**Day Seven**

The author is writing about the demonstration of good works in relation to false teachers. Again, as believers in God, there are things expected of us and one of those is service to others. Jesus did it...time and time again. If you flip through the New Testament, we find Jesus is always helping someone out, doing for others. This is who Jesus is.

This is who we need to be. Everyday. Sure, there's a need for folks to travel overseas and help provide potable water for remote villagers, but each of us should be on the lookout – constantly – for ways to help the people standing right next to us. It may be distracting a grumpy toddler so her mother can finish checking out at the grocery store. Or shoveling the sidewalk for our neighbors. Or simply giving a stranger a big ol' smile. Start looking around for these opportunities.

Reflections

Worship

Exodus 20:3
"You shall have no other God before Me"

Week Six   **Day One**

Growing up my family had some specific rules to live by. Some rules were flexible and allowed for some self-will decisions to be made. I liked those because there was some wiggle room in my attempts to defend myself when it was discovered I had broken one of them.

The specific rules were a different matter altogether. There were no excuses allowed nor was there to be any debate about the consequences that were forthcoming. Wrong was wrong in those cases, and just take what was coming like a man, or whatever.

God is not one to allow any other god before Himself. Period, end of discussion. Moses relates this commandment to God's people so that they knew worship of anything else, person, place or thing, will not be tolerated. You do not have to read far in God's Word to see He is serious about being the only God in our lives.

The false gods that we allow into our life are in direct conflict with this commandment. Money, power, prestige, sex, food, anything else but God. If you think you do not have an idol, try to stop something you are doing, see if you can. If not, it is an addiction or idol.

Reflections

Bible Reading

Luke 1:3, 4
"Having investigated everything carefully from the
beginning, to write it out for you...
that you might know the exact truth..."

Week Six   **Day Two**

We are very blessed to be living in the "communication age." With the internet, cell phones, satellite communications, TV, radio, etc.... we are able to get and receive all sorts of communications. In fact, like it or not, unless you have a communications device or two, you will be left out in the cold when it comes to being in touch with family, friends, colleges or information sharing areas. No longer is the daily newspaper, local telephone, C B radios or smoke signals the preferred method of communication between humans.

Yet, with the advances in communication, there does not mean there is an increase in the truth being transmitted. Dr. Luke of Bible fame wrote a letter to someone for the express purpose of defining the truth about certain local events. He writes, "It seems fitting for me to...write...so that you might know the exact truth." Brother Luke understood the value of having the correct understanding of Jesus and His purpose on earth, correctly disseminated. It is the Bible that contains these truths that even after all these years remain applicable and relevant for us today.

Reflections

Prayer

Genesis 20:17
"And Abraham's prayer to God, and God healed…"

Week Six   **Day Three**

There is nothing like being able to have control of events in your life. It seems like life seems to be so sweet as long as things are going our way. We base our happiness on these controlled outcomes. We attempt to grow as managers, workers, citizens and even Christians as while attempting to control our surroundings.

God certainly wants us to move toward these goals in our spiritual journey toward Him. Nevertheless, it is His option to train us or lead us any way He chooses to. Normally that means some storms will come as a way for us to grow more dependent on Him.

In this passage Abraham had lived under the protection of a foreign king for a while and during that time his wife had come to live under the king's lustful eyes. Abraham finally told him Sarah was his wife, the king released her, and Abraham prayed to God and He opened the wombs of the king's household.

Abraham had a storm in his life, partly of his own making. He prayed to God, came clean about his deception to the king and God answered his prayer. Prayer works, prayer is necessary in our spiritual growth and prayer is a privilege we have been given as children of God. Use it wisely and often!

Reflections

Meditation

Mark 1:35
"In the early morning, while…He rose and went out and
departed to a lonely place and was praying there."

Week Six   **Day Four**

Life is a rush sometimes. At times it's our own efforts that
cause it. At other times it is just life happening. Regardless, we
often get so caught up in our rush we stop doing the things
necessary to keep us in balance.

Jesus had a busy ministry. Most folks thought He was only
around to heal the sick, cast out demons, raise the dead and
various other miracles in the service of others. Those things
were part of His mission. In the gospels it is clear that those
tasks had a draining effect on Him. That part of His service on
earth caused Him to be in a rush and, not properly managed
could get Him out of balance, just like what happens to us.

Our passage today shows that He was deliberate in His
self-care. He knew His days would be busy so He would get
up "early" to commune with His Father in heaven. Jesus had
a very successful ministry, mostly because even as the Son of
God and being God Himself, He took time to meditate with
his Father.

We can do no less. There is no other way to stay close to
God and understand His will for us each day except being
with Him and allowing Him to tell us. It also allows us to rid
ourselves of the stuff that gets built up in our life.

Reflections

Physical Wellness

3 John 1:2
"I pray in all respects you may prosper
and be in good health…"

Week Six   **Day Five**

I have been having problems with pain in my shoulders. My range of motion is compromised as well as my strength in that area. Nothing is more frustrating than to try to put on my jacket and have pain shoot down my arm.

I have things I want to accomplish during the day. With this pain I end up being limited in my success. So, I do a specific exercise to strengthen my rotator cuff, use ice and anti-inflammatory aspirin. With that, I am improving my chances to be successful in my daily tasks. Self-care is a key to my ability to serve God and do His will for my life.

John opens his third letter with a prayer that his readers are in good health. Some would say he is just being polite and sociable. Partly this is true. He does understand that if they are in good health and their souls are prospering, then they would be in the correct posture before God to be capable servants. My prayer for my readers is the same, I too understand that your good health benefits God's plan.

Reflections

Fellowship

Ezekiel 11:17
"Thus says the Lord God, I shall gather you from the peoples and assemble you out of the countries among which you have been scattered…"

Week Six   **Day Six**

Nothing is more enjoyable for me than having family get-togethers. Growing up we had an annual family reunion at a farm my uncle owned. The adults would talk and reminisce and us kids would play. We youngsters would eat, play, eat, play and do so largely unsupervised. What a great time.

As I have grown up, I still look forward to family times. I have a son of my own and my siblings have children they bring around also. Now we are older and our kids are grown, but the enjoyment is still the same. Our kids are now all old enough to have their own kids, where does the time go?

God knows the value of His people coming back together. He is going to gather them back from all the places they have migrated to. The fellowship of His people brings Him joy. He knows they are better together than being separated. Purposeful fellowship makes God happy and is part of His plan for our lives.

Reflections

Service

Mark 1:13
"And He was in the wilderness forty days being tempted by Satan…and the angels were ministering to Him."

Week Six   **Day Seven**

This is one of my favorite stories in the Bible. It has always fascinated me that Jesus had to be served at all. He was the Son of God and it seems that He would be self-sufficient. Why would He need to be tended to by anyone. The most remarkable part of the story is that Satan was able to just roll up on the Son of God anytime he wanted.

He was fully God and He was fully human. He could have provided for Himself after His long commune with His Father in the wilderness. So, I have to bore down and look for the lesson in this passage.

One of the lessons is that we all need to be served at times. God wants us to be dependent on Him always. He wants to provide for us. It's not that we are totally inept and cannot help ourselves. He gives us gifts and abilities to do just that. He is our Father and wants to help, be part of our life and success story.

I am the worst about trying to be independent. I need to allow others to help, call friends when in need and bless others with my service. I am getting better but have a ways to go. God sent angels to aide His Son, He will send us help as well. He will also send us; we need to let Him.

Reflections

Worship

Exodus 20:5
"I, the Lord your God, am a jealous God."

Week SevenDay One

God has made it perfectly clear that we are to worship Him—and Him alone—and makes no bones about letting us know that He is possessive of the worship belonging to Him. This verse, part of the Ten Commandments, speaks directly to idolatry of the ancient world, but it also speaks directly to idolatry today. Idolatry refers to anyone or anything that steal our hearts from God. This can be money or people or prestige or popularity on social media.

God will not stand for us to turn our sights to anyone/anything other than Him. Period. He makes it clear that He is jealous. So when we worship, it had best be with God. And often.

Reflections

Bible Reading

Mark 4:33b
"…He was speaking the word to them as they were able to hear it."

Week Seven   **Day Two**

God speaks to us on our level. Throughout the Bible, Jesus used parables to illustrate His points. He did this so that the listeners could understand. He spoke their language. And He speaks ours. As we go through the year with this book, we will see all the different ways God communicates with us. We just need to learn to hear.

The Bible gives us countless examples of all the different ways God allows us to hear him. And He uses different methods for different people in different circumstances. I have read through the entire Bible countless times and I don't know how many times I've come across Scripture that I don't ever remember reading and wonder when my Bible was updated with a newer version! It's not a newer version, of course, but it is God opening my heart up to a particular thought/idea/lesson He needs me to hear. If we spend time in the Word, God will speak to us through it.

Reflections

Prayer

Psalms 6:9
"The Lord has heard my supplication; the Lord has heard
my prayer."

Week Seven   **Day Three**

Again, the Bible is brimming with examples of God hearing
the prayers of others…as He will ours. Here, David, in this
individual lament psalm, is conveying his concern that God
uses His adversaries to punish him, but more importantly,
expresses confidence that God will answer his prayer.

This is so important for us: to know, really know, that
our Lord and Savior is hanging on to every word we utter to
Him. He wants us to talk with Him and share all our fears and
hopes and every little thought we have. Prayer is intimate and
oh so personal and we need to know that we are being heard.
He is listening.

Reflections

Meditation

John 3:27
"A man can receive nothing unless it has been given him from heaven."

John the Baptist is watching as he is "losing" people because they are drawn to Jesus. I'm afraid, if in the same situation, I might feel a bit jealous. Not John. He realizes that God is the one who is in control, not him. John also is fully aware that his purpose – what has been given to him from heaven – is to help attract sinners to Jesus. Which he is doing!! So, this actually becomes a "win" for John the Baptist!

I wonder how many times we don't see the "win" in our own lives because we are so focused on others looking better than us or seemingly more successful than we are. I have come to realize, in my own life, that God's assignments for me tend to be the ones behind the scenes – the inglorious, rarely appreciated, but oh, so needed tasks. I have also come to appreciate the fact that these missions are truly critical. So I am able – sometimes – to forego the jealousy of the one getting all the attention and kudos and sit back and enjoy the fact that I was 1) obedient to God, and 2) a critical part. And then be grateful to God for the chance to be a part of something He needed done.

Reflections

Physical Wellness

Jeremiah 30:17
"For I will restore you to health,
I will heal you of your wounds."

Week Seven   **Day Five**

Jeremiah is talking about the future when God restores Israel and offers up the blessings of His new covenant. Here we see that physical wellness is a part of those blessings: that is how important our physical well-being is to God.

Which begs the questions: Why do I have cancer? Why has God allowed me to suffer with MS? Why do I only have one leg? We are told, time after time, in His Word that afflictions and sufferings are part of life and that Christians are to use these times to draw closer to God and be a beacon for those with similar burdens.

But I digress. Since our bodies are the homes of our Holy Spirits – and likened to temples (1Cor 6:19) – we still must take the utmost care of them. Believe me, I'm not particularly crazy about this because I struggle with addictions that are not good for me and I can really destroy some ice cream! But then I have to remember who lives here – both my Holy Spirit and me! My home may need some repairs, but it always, always, always is clean and well taken care of...why is it so hard for me to have this same attitude about my body?

Reflections

Fellowship

Mark 2:15
"…many tax-gatherers and sinners were dining with Jesus
and His disciples; for there were many of them…"

Week Seven   **Day Six**

Jesus spent a whole lot of time with people of questionable reputations. In fact, I believe that Jesus preferred to hang out with the outcasts of his time. And He caught a lot of flak about it as well. The Pharisees certainly had much to say about Jesus' dinner mates! But Jesus saw people through their needs – not their stereotypes – and through these "sinners," He showed us how to be a living example of the "will of God."

We humans simply are afraid of people who sin differently from us and refuse to have anything to do with them. This is not what Jesus taught or modelled. We need to remember to fellowship – investing time - with others that are different from us. Obviously, we need to have constant contact with fellow Christians but like Jesus examples, there are those who need to know His love.

Reflections

Service

1 Kings 18:4
"Obadiah took a hundred prophets and hid them by fifties
in a cave and provided them with bread and water."

Week Seven   **Day Seven**

Service sometimes means doing for others we don't particularly get along with or even agree with. Service sometimes means providing for someone when we aren't sure how to provide for ourselves. Service sometimes means putting ourselves in uncomfortable situations. Service often times means stepping out of our comfort zones.

The good news is that every time we humble ourselves to help or provide for or do for another person – Christians and non-Christians alike – we are sitting smack dab in God's will. What a wonderful place that is!

Reflections

Worship

Revelation 4:10
"Twenty-four elders will fall down before Him who sits on the throne, and will worship Him who lives forever..."

Week Eight   **Day One**

If you have ever watched any of the "Indiana Jones" movies, the ones starring Harrison Ford, he is always searching for some timeless relic. In the movie there are always scenes where he is secretly watching some sort of native tribal ritual. The natives are all dancing and bowing down to a king, leader or idol. Music is playing, chanting is being done and great reverence is being shown.

Now those are movies and based on fiction novels. Nevertheless, the imagery shows the custom of worship. I often think how crazy it is to worship that way. Yet, I am so pious I only worship solemnly and, in my pew, reverently. I am never really putting my all into it: body, voice, heart and soul. Natives or not, those scenes show worship.

In John's book of Revelation, he tells us the elders in heaven fall down and worship Jesus. These are the guys that normally are sitting on the thrones around the throne of God. They get out of their seats and fall down before God because there is really no other way to show the respect to the Author, Creator and Savior of the universe.

Reflections

Bible Reading

John 8:31
"Jesus was therefore saying…if you abide in My word then you are truly disciples of mine."

Week Eight   **Day Two**

There is a difference in "knowing" what to do and actually "doing" what is right. There is a quote that says, "The road to hell is paved with good intentions." So much of our life is filled with what we want to do, what we should do or what we feel is the right thing to do. Yet, so much is left undone, right? We make plans and never get around to acting on them. We have desires but stay in the same old rut rather than move forward toward success.

God's Word is meant to be applied to our life, it is not theory or irrelevant in today's world. John 8:31 quotes Jesus when He says, "If you abide in My Word then you are truly disciples of mine." It is not enough to say, plan or intend to be obedient to God's Word. Jesus says that we actually have to practice the principles He lays out in the Bible and through the example of His life.

Reflections

Prayer

Matthew 6:8,9
"Your Father knows what you need, before you ask Him,
pray then in this way…"

Week Eight   **Day Three**

I grew up in a loving Christian home. We went to church, learned to tithe and prayed often. As a child I never really saw the need for prayer, I just did what I was told. I learned the prayers a lot of kids in church learn and recited them when asked or it was my turn at the supper table.

My parents, however, knew the value of prayer. They were constantly reminding us to pray and relating to us when prayers were answered. We learned that God does teach us about prayer and to be mindful to watch for His answer.

Our verse today is part of what the scholars call the Sermon on the Mount. Jesus is asked how to pray by one of His followers. They had seen Him pray and were witness to the mighty results. What follows is a model of how we should pray. Every preacher has broken these verses down for their congregation.

Most importantly, this model shows that there is a way to pray that is acceptable to God. James 4:3 says, "You ask and do not receive because you ask wrongly." God wants us to communicate with Him, so we must learn to approach Him correctly.

Reflections

Meditation

Psalms 104:34
"Let my meditation be pleasing to Him, as for me I shall be glad in the Lord."

Week Eight   **Day Four**

We all have had bosses before. Some are easy to get along with and some not so much. Like them or not, they are in charge and it is our responsibility to please them. I was always taught to learn what your superiors like and dislike. This is often easier said than done, but necessary in order to get along.

To do this takes some effort. It takes time to learn the ways and thoughts of your boss. In my experience the effort has always been worth it. The workplace becomes more bearable and whatever position I was in became more productive.

The psalmist in this verse is telling us to do just that. We need to spend time with God for many reasons. Mostly we do so to be pleasing to Him. It brings pleasure to God when we talk and listen to Him. We can actually "be pleasing to Him." It takes practice and probably perfection will never be achieved, but the effort to do so is honored by Him.

Reflections

Physical Wellness

Luke 13:13
"And He laid hands upon her; and immediately she was made erect again and began glorifying God."

Week Eight   **Day Five**

Hardly a day goes by when I do not run into someone who has a physical ailment. Sometimes it is a big one, sometimes just the sniffles. Every time I do so I thank God my battles with illness have been few and minor. I have been so blessed to have been healthy thus far in my life.

When my son came along it was always excruciating to see him sick. I was pastoring in a small southeastern town in Virginia when he was young. He got flu-like symptoms but no matter what I gave him he stayed ill. Finally, I took him to the local clinic and it was determined that he had strep. He received a shot and in hours he was better, what a relief.

Jesus cared about those who were not physically well. Time and time again crowds gathered around Him because they knew He cared about them. He healed folks constantly, so much in fact He had to deliberately just move on so He could actually preach. God cares about our physical wellness so we should practice self-care and help others as well in their efforts to stay well.

Reflections

Fellowship

Joshua 6:5
"It shall be that when they make a long blast with the ram's horn…all the people will shout with a great shout…"

Week Eight   **Day Six**

I love the stories of Joshua's conquering of the Promised Land. They are full of mighty acts of God and obedience of His people. The reward is within their grasp and now all they have to do is work together to seize it.

Joshua had sent spies ahead to scout out the city of Jericho. They reported back about the city and the fear the inhabitants had of the people of God. With all the logistical data collected, Joshua leads God's people to defeat the city.

Most battle generals would not have chosen to attack the way God had planned. God told them to march around the city and on a certain day and time to "shout." As one group, they did so, and the walls of the city came tumbling down. Amazing, right?

God let them know then and wants us to know now that the fellowship, singly minded, is powerful. Just as powerful as Joshua's army was on the day the walls of Jericho came tumbling down.

Reflections

Service

Matthew 22:39
"The second is like it, you shall love your neighbor as
yourself."

Growing up I was taught in church the Golden Rule. Matthew 7:12 says that we need to treat people like we want to be treated. My parents made me treat my brother and sister in this manner. I failed miserably most of the time but did learn to understand the concept.

When asked, Jesus boiled the Ten Commandments down to these two: love God with everything you have and love your neighbor as yourself. Of all that Jesus taught while on this earth, He determined those two lessons were the most important to learn.

Seems simple enough, right? Not so much usually. The key to the second command is to serve others. If we are doing that, then we are not being selfish and self-centered. We are giving, not demanding to receive. We are putting ourselves in a humble position before God. Service works to put us on a spiritual path that pleases God.

Reflections

Worship

Revelation 4:10b
"Worship Him who lives for ever and ever."

Week Nine   **Day One**

In Revelation 4:10, the twenty-four elders fall down before Him - who sits on the throne, who lives for ever and ever - and worship Him. This is another example of the Scriptures instructing us to worship. It is that important. And this passage reiterates that we are to worship the God who will never go away. He will never leave us; we will never outlive Him. He is, and will be, always there for us.

Worship doesn't always mean we throw ourselves on the ground; in fact, worshipping God comes in so many different forms. Throughout this year, we will see countless examples of how to worship. The important thing to remember is that we actually do worship the Everlasting King.

Reflections

Bible Reading

Acts 8:35
"Philip opened his mouth and beginning from this Scripture
he preached Jesus to him."

Week Nine   **Day Two**

Dr. Mayson writes in *When Life Shows Up:* "Not everything we read, hear, watch or see in our in-boxes is true". The world is full of "spam"- information that is not wanted, designed for sensationalism or offered for the purpose of appealing to our overactive egos. All this information, no matter what it is called is offered in an attempt to shape our thinking, spread a specific agenda or sell us something we really do not need. Obviously, there is some truth out there in the information portals but it has to be sifted to be found.

So what are we Christians to do? Do we sell our communication devices and rely on God to funnel all necessary information into our brains, then allow it to move to our hearts? Sounds good, right, nevertheless there is so much "white noise" in our heads a lot would be missed. In the Book of Acts 8:35, Luke writes, "Philip opened his mouth and beginning from Scripture…" That's the answer folks, begin in scripture. With the teachings of the Bible as our filter we can begin to hear the message, from any source that God intends for us to hear.

Reflections

Prayer

John 14:14
"If you ask Me anything in My name, I will do it."

Week Nine   **Day Three**

Anything? The winning lottery ticket? The demise of an archenemy? A pass on a heinous crime we've been accused of, but didn't commit? Not exactly. God wants us to come to Him for everything. He wants us to be able to ask Him for anything. That's the whole reason for prayer – letting down our defenses, coming before Him broken, hurting, scared, hopeful, honest.

This can be a tough one, but as we grow and mature in our relationship with Christ, we learn that our prayers need to line up with the will of Him. To pray in Jesus' name is to pray in accordance to God's will and glory. So, not all our prayers are going to be answered in the way we want them to – especially those that go against God's nature. But I guarantee that every prayer we utter is heard by God.

Reflections

Meditation

2 Kings 20:3
"I beseech Thee, O Lord, remember now how I have walked
before Thee in truth and with a perfect heart,
and have done that which is good in Thy sight.
And Hezekiah wept bitterly."

Week Nine   **Day Four**

In 2 Kings 20 we find that Hezekiah has become gravely ill. Isaiah shows up and tells him to "get his house in order" because Hezekiah is about to die. What does Hezekiah (or any human, for that matter!) do? He immediately goes to God and begs, pleads, points out all the good stuff he's done – all the things we do when our butts are on fire. And then Hezekiah "wept bitterly." I get it. He simply wasn't ready to die.

In the end, God sends Isaiah back to Hezekiah to tell him that he will be healed. What I love about this little story is that Hezekiah was in that dark, scary place – the place where we feel paralyzing fear and utter hopelessness and crushing despair. And the first place he goes is the only place he could get any relief and comfort – God. It is during these horrible times that God can show us His mercy and grace, as long as we actually go to Him, trust Him, let Him do what He does best. He ALWAYS comes through.

Reflections

Physical Wellness

Psalms 38:3b
"There is no health in my bones because of my sin…"

Week Nine Day Five

As we talk about physical wellness as a spiritual discipline, not only are there things we should be doing, but there are also things we shouldn't be doing. We need to look at what causes physical un-wellness. Of course, sometimes it is simply because we caught a cold or strained a muscle or broke a bone. But carrying hate in our hearts or ill-will towards others can also cause physical sickness.

How many times have we endured the tension headache because we are stressed about something, we cannot do anything about? David wrote (in this lamenting Psalm) that because of his sin, his body is suffering. We, too, have all experienced this same sickness. In order to maintain our physical wellness, along with exercise, eating right, etc., we need to acknowledge the impact sinning against God has on us physically.

Reflections

Fellowship

Deuteronomy 6:6,7
"These words which I am commanding you today…you shall teach them diligently to your sons…"

Week Nine   **Day Six**

When I think of fellowship, I think about hanging out in the Fellowship Hall of my church, talking with other people. Or sharing a potluck meal with the ladies of the church. Or ministering to the homeless in my town. But fellowship also requires us to have a relationship with our children in which regular instructions of God's will is taught.

It is so easy to miss this: in our busy lives, we get so wrapped up in schedules and activities and commitments and homework, that it is very easy to forget fellowshipping with our kids. This is such a powerful time in which we can show our children how important they are to us. And to God. Enforce daily meals in which all members of the family sit down, eat, and fellowship. Put those phones away. Turn off the TV. And listen.

Reflections

Service

John 13:14
"If then the Lord and Teacher washed your feet, you also ought to wash one another's feet."

Week Nine   **Day Seven**

Feet washing. That's a tough one for me as I do not like feet. Not mine and certainly not someone else's. And yet, I'm told that I am to wash the feet of another because Jesus did. Now, I certainly understand that this verse means we are to humble ourselves and, in a spirit of humility, serve one another. And some service activities are very easy for me but, obviously, others are not.

The point is, Jesus – our Lord, our Savior, our King – regularly, and without hesitation, humbled himself to others. He modeled how we are to serve those around us with love. And by thinking of others before thinking of self, we find ourselves at the heart of service. If Jesus did it, then so should I. Even feet washing.

Reflections

Worship

Psalms 66:4
"All the earth will worship Thee, and will sing praises to
Thee, they will sing praises to Thy name."

Week Ten   **Day One**

Growing up my family had a house on a large lake. Most of the vacations we took were at this lake. We water skied, fished, had picnics on the boat and just enjoyed ourselves. Even after becoming an adult with a kid of my own I went to this lake for vacation. It was a place that several generations grew to enjoy.

As I look back on that time, I remember very few unpleasant moments. My siblings and I talk often of the fond times there. When anyone begins to talk about their favorite place, this lake house is always mine. I just want to tell everyone what a great place that was for me.

This Psalm reminds me of the desire to tell the whole world about my special place and how God allowed my family to find such peace and joy at that lake. In this Psalm, the author is praising God for some national deliverance of His people. I want to always praise God for the events in my life. He controls them all and is worthy of my praise. Get started today making a choice to praise God for all He does for you.

Reflections

Bible Reading

Romans 16:25, 26
Now to Him who is able to establish you according to my
gospel and the preaching of Jesus Christ...
now is manifested and by the Scriptures...
has been made know to all the nations..."

Week Ten   **Day Two**

One thing for certain is that positive strides in our spiritual development do not come accidentally. In fact, nothing good in life that is lasting comes out of the blue. Sitting around wishing for "good luck" or hanging around waiting for your "ship to come in" never happens. You can wait all you want but until you make some sort of effort, the mysteries of true happiness will always stay elusive.

In God's economy, the route to peace and happiness is truly made available only to those who seek them. Paul, in his epistle to the church in Rome, lets us know in Romans 16:25, 26 that, "Now to Him who is able to establish you...according to the revelation of the mystery which has been kept secret for long past ages." These secrets are revealed to us through "the Scriptures," not from info-mercials or the daily news sources. God wants us to have the information we need but wants us to seek it from the correct information sources and that is His Word.

Reflections

Prayer

Act 4:31
"When they had prayed the place where they had gathered together was shaken and they were all filled with the Holy Spirit…"

Week Ten   **Day Three**

Peter and John had run into some problems with the local religious rulers. These short-sighted religious types put them in jail because they did not like what these men of God were teaching. They were upset because what was being said confronted their selfish and self-serving ways.

After being released from jail, Peter and John were warned not to keep doing what they were doing, telling others about the saving Good News of Jesus' death on the cross. Our heroes answered that they could not stop telling others what they had seen and heard.

Gathered together again with fellow believers, they began to pray and this great event happened. The Holy Spirit filled those who were there. Prayer does that. Great things happen as a result. Do not let anyone deter you from your prayer life. Be expectant, look for mighty results in your prayer life.

Reflections

Meditation

2 Samuel 7:18
"Then David the king went in and sat before the Lord...
Who am I Lord God..."

Week Ten   **Day Four**

Most of us were taught growing up that if you wanted anything you had to work for it. There are no free meals in life, everything must be earned. The early bird gets the worm and there is no place in life for a lazy person.

Some folks even go so far as to say that we, internally, have all the power to make ourselves successful. We can pull ourselves up by our own bootstraps and change our situation. Our own inner strength just needs to be harnessed correctly for us to succeed.

In this passage we read some real truths about these statements. King David sat before God understanding that all he had came from God. David was obedient and worked hard but he knew there was nothing he had that God did not give to Him.

Meditating before God helps us understand who we are in God's grand design. Getting personal, alone with God, clears up faulty notions of our own grand abilities. Taking a little time with God yields great clarity.

Reflections

Physical Wellness

Proverbs 19:24
"The sluggard buries his hand in the dish…"

Week Ten   **Day Five**

The greatest joy of my life has been being a father. I was blessed to have a son to whom I could give of myself to, and I found that it completed me. It was not an easy job at times, but every bit of energy I expended helping him to grow into the fine young man he is today was worth it.

I obviously give God most of the credit. I give my parents a lot of credit also because I kind of did just what they did for me. Countless hours I spent throwing one kind of ball or another with my Dad and also working alongside him doing projects somewhere or another. We had innumerable dinner table discussions about life and Bible studies.

I did the same for my son. Parenting is an active sport, not one done well by a coach potato. In my house growing up and in my own adult home there was no yelling or snapping in forms of correction. There was always hands on, loving, Godly uses of discipline.

A sluggard does not have that kind of stamina. A sluggard does not have the physical ability to be completely involved in life. A sluggard whiles away their time with useless and meaningless activity. The results are not good for them or those around them and certainly not a Godly posture.

Reflections

Fellowship

Luke 2:8,10
"In the same region there were some shepherds staying out in the fields, keeping watch over their flock…"

Week Ten   **Day Six**

In the days this passage was written shepherds were not considered very highly. They did not abide by the normal ceremonial schedules or stay ritualistically clean. They did not participate in the feasts or pal around with the religious rulers of the day. They were considered outcasts.

Yet, their job was very important. Even Jesus is called the Good Shepherd. The care and protection they offered their flocks was essential. Sheep, by themselves could do nothing to keep themselves alive. The shepherds did it all.

To do so they had to work together. The job was exhausting and continual. Even at night they had to be at work. There had to be a fellowship of workers so this gigantic task could get done.

We Christians need to take a lesson from these humble workers. We are not designed to do this life journey alone. God made us herd people, dependent on each other for survival.

Reflections

Service

Proverbs 11:2
"When pride comes, then comes dishonor; but with the humble is wisdom."

Week Ten   **Day Seven**

I remember being in the fourth grade going out to look at the stars with my Dad. My Dad was one of the smartest people I have ever known. For some reason I was in the habit, in my young life, of saying "I know."

Obviously, being a fourth grader, I knew very little. I am not sure why I was even saying this around such a smart man. Nevertheless, I did and he was not happy with my assumptions about my knowledge.

That night he made it clear that nobody likes a "know-it-all." He told me that kind of person falsely thinks too much of themselves and gives little respect to those around him. He said if you truly want to be wise then you will have to learn to be humble.

Of course, I did not make much of it then, being a genius and all. As I look back, what a valuable lesson. I grow up, begin to study God's Word and He tells me the same thing. I cannot be of service if I put myself above others. I am not usable by God with this defeating approach on life. I get it today, thanks Dad.

Reflections

Worship

Psalms 66:16
"Come and hear all who fear God and I will tell of what He
has done for my soul."

Week Eleven   **Day One**

This is one of the perks of worshipping: we get to hear how
God works in others' lives. We get to see what God is capable
of and, especially when we are in periods of doubt, we build
our hope as to His goodness. Worship bolsters us. It shows us
that the promises of God actually do happen.

The flip of this is that when we worship, we also get to
share what God has done "for our soul" in order to give hope to
others. We have all been in the place where we wonder if God
really does hear us and if He really does care. By hearing (and
sharing) of his goodness and faithfulness, our doubt dissipates
and our souls are restored!

Reflections

Bible Reading

Romans 10:17
"So faith comes from hearing and hearing by the Word
of God."

Week Eleven   **Day Two**

It is funny what we are willing to repeat or pass from one person to another. We all get caught up in passing along stories either by word of mouth, internet or cell phone. We do not bother checking the facts, we just click forward on our communication devices and share with others. Not all of it is harmful but very little of it leads to personal growth. Shamefully, if examined, our words are predominately just empty rhetoric used just to fill the silence.

Imagine if we intentionally made it our purpose to share only information that helps make those around us better people. It does not have to be deep, philosophical, mental gymnastics but just life lessons. Paul gives us a good topic in Romans 10:17. He says, "Faith comes from hearing and hearing by the Word of Christ." The Bible is a goldmine of useful, practical information. The Words shared from this Holy Book will lead our brothers and sisters of the world to a place of faith, peace and contentment. That, folks, beats gossip around the water cooler.

Reflections

Prayer

Philippians 1:3-4
"I thank my God in all my remembrance of you, always offering prayer with joy in my every prayer for you all."

Week Eleven   **Day Three**

This was written when Paul was imprisoned. Paul mentions prayer twice – that's significant. Prayer is not only used to petition God but is to be used to praise God and the goodness – including other people – in our lives. There is something very powerful about praying for others. We are told to do it. Jesus did it. And it can transform our relationships with others.

The second part of this passage says that we are to pray with joy. That can be hard sometimes when we are praying for a difficult person (or even for one we simply cannot stand!). But I promise you, praying with joy for someone that we are struggling with truly changes the way we feel about that person. Try it! You'll see.

Reflections

Meditation

1 Samuel 19:23b
"…the Spirit of God came upon him also…"

Week Eleven   **Day Four**

So, when Saul sends his messengers to Naioth to take David, God sends His Spirit upon those messengers, which in turns enables them to prophesy. God does amazing things when we let Him. His power is unbelievable and without limits. When we open our hearts and minds and enter His presence, He can – and will – do amazing things. He will enlighten us, empower us, comfort us, love us, and even give us super-human abilities sometimes! But we have to show up.

Reflections

Physical Wellness

Romans 1:24
"God gave them over in the lusts of their hearts to impurity,
so that their bodies might dishonor them."

Week Eleven   **Day Five**

God allows us to make choices. Even bad ones. That's what the whole sin/forgiveness of sin/Jesus dying on the cross for our sins is all about. He also gives us the most awesome gifts. In the Scripture today, the gift we are talking about is sex. God is very clear about his expectations of our choices when it comes to sex and He is equally clear about the consequences of making bad decisions regarding sex. Our Creator made us to desire and enjoy sex and He knows that we are sinful by nature, a bad combo.

Here, Paul is illustrating the progressiveness of human unrighteousness and how rejecting one facet of God can cause additional rejections of Him. As a result, we must be ever diligent about our actions, thoughts, words. When we don't, it seems that we become immune and, over time, become okay with that which is not righteous. It's progressive. What was once unacceptable is not only accepted but embraced and even celebrated. This is why we must know what the Bible says, follow what it says, and be accountable for what it says.

Reflections

Fellowship

2 Chronicles 7:14
"If my people who are called by My name humble
themselves and pray and seek My face and turn from their
wicked ways, then I will hear from heaven and will forgive
their sin and heal their land."

Week Eleven   **Day Six**

The overall, larger context of 2 Chronicles 7 is talking about Israel and the temple and how, occasionally, God sends judgment in the form of drought or locust on the land. Since God entered into His covenant with all of Israel, He would not only deal with individuals, but also the group as a whole, the fellowship. God is a relational being. And He expects us to be as well. There will be times when God will look down on a church or small group or Sunday school class and become concerned or displeased with what's going on.

This is another reason fellowship is so important. God expects us to come together often and practice, if you will, our tenets and beliefs and ways on each other. I suppose He does this so that we can hone our skills; when we are with unbelievers, our behavior and attitude will be in line with Christ's. Kind of brings a new perspective to your next fellowship experience, huh?

Reflections

Service

Luke 6:38
"Give and it will be given to you. They will pour into your lap a good measure…For by your standard of measure it will be measure to you in return."

Week Eleven   **Day Seven**

This should not be the reason we do service work, but this verse promises us that there are indeed awards for it and, in fact, these rewards will match our endeavors. Service is almost always inconvenient, time-consuming, and tends to take us out of our comfort zones. However, I don't think I've ever been of service to others where I don't walk away feeling better, more rewarded, and more satisfied than those that are on the receiving side.

Additionally, those rewards always give a glimpse of the nature of our Father. When we give, we see God's love and generosity and faithfulness – we get to see God, Himself. I don't know about you but giving up an afternoon helping someone less fortunate than me and being rewarded by seeing God seems to be an opportunity of a lifetime. Oh, and beware: it is addicting!

Reflections

Worship

Philippians 3:3
"For we are the true circumcision, who worship in the Spirit of God and glory in Christ Jesus and put no confidence in the flesh."

Week Twelve   **Day One**

Developing spiritual disciplines is like lifting weights. You start light and work yourself up in weight. But weight increase is not the only goal. Form is part of body development. You must lift correctly to target certain muscles and not to damage others. Since it is a lifestyle change you are developing, there is no rush in it. Many folks start things and do not finish because they take on too much and frustrate themselves with lack of results.

Paul is helping us to understand here that the prize of the Christian life is the true knowledge of God. We will know that we are on target with our goal if our worship is only of God and we care not about what others think, say or do about it. So take it slow, develop a lifestyle of worship, be realistic in your expectations and be God focused. Keep up the good work, readers!

Reflections

Bible Reading

Psalms 119:105
"Thy Word is a lamp unto my feet and a light to my path."

Week Twelve   **Day Two**

Anyone who has ever been camping knows how important a flashlight is. It is all good while everyone is awake and the cook fire is still burning, casting off plenty of illumination. Everyone retires to their tents, the fire dies and sure enough you need to go to the bathroom. When you open the tent flap and peek out, it is so dark. No streetlights or illumination from buildings, cars or even the moon. Dark.

You get the picture. As an aviator I was taught how far a pilot, in certain conditions, could see a single beacon of light on the ground. It was astounding. Like camping, flying in the dark of night could get very challenging. It was always a relief when I would see the column of runway lights begin to appear.

This is exactly what the Psalmist is saying. God's Word does that for us. It is the directional beacon we can follow that guides us to God, His will and spiritual development. His light is necessary because it is the only way we can maneuver through life and still be in the correct posture before Him.

Reflections

Prayer

Romans 8:26
"We do not know how to pray as we should,
but the Spirit Himself intercedes for us with
groanings too deep for words."

Week Twelve   **Day Three**

There has been time in my life when I was so beat down, I did not know how to proceed. I did not even know where to begin to start to move forward. I was in such a place - foreign and unfamiliar - there were no landmarks to guide me to God's plan, His purpose or His help. Lost is even too small to describe my condition. These times came when I was a Pastor, so I felt my spiritual condition was good, yet lost is what I was.

What could I pray for? How do I approach this gigantic task? How will I survive this unreal event? These were some of my questions. Thankfully, I know God knows where I am and what I am going through. He provided me the Holy Spirit to do for me what I could not do for myself.

All I could do is groan for I had no words, no idea or no light to follow. The Holy Spirit knew my needs, knew God's plan and provided me with the next step, and the next and the next until I could ascertain for myself how to move forward. Praise God and the privilege of prayer.

Reflections

Meditation

Ruth 3:18
"Wait my daughter, until you know how the matter
turns out..."

Week Twelve   **Day Four**

Part of growing and developing good spiritual disciplines is learning to wait on God's answer. We want everything right now or yesterday. We get in a hurry in the spiritual pursuits of our life to get God's next step or answer. Common mistake for even the best of Christians.

Here Ruth has been led by her mother-in-law, Naomi, to wait for the answer that Boaz would bring. One of the greatest love stories ever is the relationship between Ruth and Naomi. Naomi wants Ruth to tie her future up with the successful, godly Boaz. Ruth has done that and now it is time to wait to see what Boaz will do.

It's not an easy task to wait. The alternative is to rush ahead of God and possibly mess things up. The discipline of meditation - listening for God - will solve a lot of issues with misdirection in our lives. As mentioned earlier in this devotional, Oswald Chambers says that we need not pray for an answer from God but to pray for contact with Him.

Reflections

Physical Wellness

Ephesians 3:20
"To Him who is able to do exceedingly abundantly beyond
all we ask or think according to the power that works
within us."

Week Twelve   **Day Five**

Not many folks talk about physical wellness when they think
of spiritual disciplines. I do not know why because keeping our
vessel usable for God is so important. All the good intentions
in the world to follow God as directed are no good if our
bodies are broken. Obviously, there is nothing we can do about
disease or genetic issues we have. Mostly that is not the issue,
we just do not make our self-care a priority.

Paul is helping us understand in this passage that we have
an unlimited resource to accomplish what is asked of us. We
have to put in the effort and "the power that works within us"
will do the rest. He is being encouraging to his readers. He
wants them to know they have supernatural help. Do what
is asked and be astounded by what the results can be. Rely
on God, be obedient and see how He works. Take care of
the vessel God gave you for His purpose and He will use you
mightily. God wants us to develop good self-care so we can
be useful to Him. More so, we can be at peace with ourselves.

Reflections

Fellowship

Ezra 3:10
"When the builders had laid the foundation…the Levites…
with cymbals praise the Lord…"

Week Twelve **Day Six**

Fellowship is such a necessary spiritual discipline. God made us to be supportive of one another. He gave us all abilities to be shared with a group. Nobody has all they need. There has to be give and take to accomplish our spiritual journey.

God told Adam it was not good for him to be alone. From that time forward the need for others in our life was established. Later we see the family unit as the basic building block for our personal growth. Fathers and mothers and relatives were needed to raise the next generations.

In our passage today we see the Levites, as a group, banding together to celebrate the beginning of the rebuilding of the temple of God. Not just one Levite was assigned to pull this off, all of them knew it was important for them to participate in this wonderful celebration. We see this throughout God's Word; everybody was expected to participate in the assigned celebrations. Every capable male had to attend the feast as ascribed by the law.

We need to adopt this into our spiritual discipline development. We are not able to grow alone. We need each other to get better. The journey is much more peaceful when shared with the fellowship of God.

Reflections

Service

Romans 2:4
"Do you think lightly of the riches of His kindness, and forbearance and patience, not knowing that the kindness of God leads you to repentance?"

Week Twelve   **Day Seven**

"Yes sir, no sir, no excuse sir," were the only answers you could give during my Knob year at the Citadel. I went to a military college in Charleston, South Carolina. I wanted to be an Army officer like my Dad, and this was my first step.

We learned that rules were rules for a reason and that there was no excuse for breaking them. There was no special permission for what we "thought" might be a better way. You were to do what you were taught and do not think you are above everyone else who is trying to be obedient. You are not special!

Service is a must in our spiritual discipline tool kit. There will be no excuse accepted when we have to answer for going it our own way. Paul is letting the folks in Rome know exactly that. Good intentions or not, you must do it God's way. Here he offers a hypothetical question in which he implies the answer is no.

In our case we are commanded to serve others. No excuses, no "better" plan we develop will be acceptable. God's way is the only safe and successful way being in the correct posture before Him.

Reflections

Worship

Philippians 2:11
"And that every tongue will confess that Jesus Christ is
Lord..."

Week Thirteen   **Day One**

Paul was in prison when he wrote this. Can you imagine? Being in prison and still praising Jesus Christ? Paul tells the Philippian Christians that his time in prison actually afforded him the chance to witness to others – both fellow inmates and the guards. That's some powerful worship.

And that's exactly what we're expected to do in "real life." Dr. Mayson was falsely accused and convicted of a crime, spending six years in prison. While this wasn't his "favorite duty assignment," he'll be the first to tell you that God could have stopped the process anytime, but didn't because He needed Charlie to witness in the presence of other inmates and guards. That's some powerful worship.

Reflections

Bible Reading

Proverbs 30:5
"Every Word of God is tested; He is a shield to those who
take refuge in Him."

Week Thirteen   **Day Two**

The world is a tough place to live in. Even if the world is
not biting at your heels, our own character defects cause us
problems. Just when you think you have found peace and are
centered physically, mentally and spiritually, some character
trait raises it ugly head and bam, off center. As kids we could
count on our parents or older siblings to help when we started
to face difficulties in life. As we grow up, we are expected
to fend for ourselves. We are required by society to put on
our grown up pants and handle whatever circumstances life
presents to us.

Well that is all fine and good but it is just not that easy
at times. Life is meant to be a struggle and if faced head-on,
growth occurs. In Proverbs 30:5, the wise man writes, "Every
Word of God is tested, He is a shield to those who take refuge
in Him." Hey, sometimes we need help; in fact, more often
than not we need some sort of power greater than ourselves to
negotiate the mine fields of life. God is our refuge and strength;
His Word is the key to knowing His mind and methods. He
wants to help, we have to let Him; after all, our way seems to
leave something to be desired.

Reflections

Prayer

Ephesians 3:20
"Now to Him who is able to do far more abundantly beyond all that we ask or think, according to the power that works within us..."

Week Thirteen   **Day Three**

God is so much bigger than we ever give Him credit for. How many times have you prayed for something and God answers that prayer, plus some? When we pay attention, we will find that happens more often than not. Again, we need to remember that our prayers must line up with His will; but when they do – watch out!

I've found that I have prayed for a particular thing or outcome in a situation and certainly had in my mind what that would look like. And then God answers it, but differently from what I visualized. I can't tell you how many times I have been absolutely amazed at His response in that the answer was way more clever and abundant than I ever dreamed. That's our Lord and Savior!

Reflections

Meditation

Judges 3:20
"Ehud came to him while he was sitting alone in his cool roof chamber. And Ehud said,
'I have a message from God for you…'"

Week Thirteen   **Day Four**

Have you ever had a thought or idea or some similar input that came out of nowhere and flooded your mind and heart? I suspect oftentimes, these are from God. And have you ever had such a thing happen, but it concerned someone else? Again, probably a nudge from God. But how often do we pay attention? I'm pretty good about giving it some attention if it's about me but am very hesitant to go busting into someone's life to tell them about "a dream" I had.

God uses many methods to speak to us. We know that. We also should know that in order to properly hear and understand these messages, we have to hone our listening abilities. This comes, in part, through meditation. We must practice meditation if we want the Holy Spirit to speak to us and use us. Sometimes these messages are truly not about me, but, indeed, concerning someone else. I'm just the messenger. When God speaks, folks, we gotta listen! And then, we gotta act!

Reflections

Physical Wellness

John 2:21
"He was speaking of the temple of His body."

Week Thirteen   **Day Five**

Yikes! That's some strong language, Paul! Destroy?! God doesn't play around.

Although Paul is referring to the church as the temple of God, we know that our bodies have also been likened to God's holy temple. It all makes sense, though, and ties in together. If God's temple – regardless of whether it is represented as our bodies or the church – is destroyed, there is a hefty price to pay. After all, the temple is where God lives, it is where our Holy Spirit resides; it is the center, or home, of all that is holy.

And yet, I still continue to abuse this temple. I get so ashamed when I think about the condition of the home I provide for my Holy Spirit. Thank goodness my Holy Spirit is forgiving and can overlook a lot. But that's not the point. The point is, we must treat ourselves and our bodies as just that–the place that God lives.

Reflections

Fellowship

Esther 9:11
"In them the king granted the Jews…the right to assemble and to defend their lives…"

Week Thirteen   **Day Six**

We are relational creatures, even those of us who tend towards "introverted-ness." It is shown that we humans do need some sort of interaction and contact with other humans. We need that interaction to uplift us, to support us, to hold us accountable. God, too, is a relational being. And He made us in His image. So, it would stand to reason that God intended us to come together as the body of Christ and provide those relational entities.

Again, this is why fellowshipping with one another is so important. At least weekly, we must come together to uplift, support, and center ourselves with those who also follow Christ. If you haven't found a church, keep looking. If you have found a church, get involved. Talk with others. Introduce yourself. It's really important.

Reflections

Service

1 Thessalonians 1:3
"Constantly bearing in mind your work of faith and labor of love and steadfastness of hope...."

Week Thirteen   **Day Seven**

"Constantly bearing in mind...." What a wonderful way to approach our lives: always on the lookout for opportunities to demonstrate faith and love and hope. It is absolutely amazing how a simple act of kindness or a genuinely encouraging word can change the day – and even the life – of someone our path crosses. This is the way Jesus lived his life: always looking to enhance the lives of those around us.

We spend way too much time being negative and tearing others down who don't agree with us, look different from us, don't sin the way we do. And the anonymity that social media affords allows us to be quick to condemn. Paul praises the Christians at Thessalonica for demonstrating their faith and points out that through the work of the Holy Spirit and their attentiveness, amazing changes in their lives occur. I challenge you to "constantly bear in mind" your duty to be of service to others. Watch how it impacts you!

Reflections

Worship

Genesis 1:27
"God created man in His own image, in the image of God
He created him…"

Week Fourteen   **Day One**

On God's last workday He made His greatest creation, man. It
has long been a topic of discussion of what is meant by "in His
own image." It is said twice for emphasis here in this passage.
Even after saying it twice there is no real consensus on what
it means. I do know that God is our role model and there is
something in us that draws us to be closer to Him. He wants
us near Him and to function in a way that glorifies Him. We
tend to be like Him if we are moving in the correct spiritual
direction.

I have never worried about that question. I have just always
been glad God made us. As we read through His Word, we
find that we are special to Him. He loves us. He even sent His
Son to die for our sins. He did this so we can have a better
relationship with Him.

The bottom line for me is that God is worthy to be
praised. Everything He does is for our own good. He created
everything that there is and wants us to be blessed by it all.
The need to worship God is the only real take away from the
confusing verse.

Reflections

Bible Reading

Isaiah 5:24
"For they have rejected the law of the Lord of hosts…"

Week Fourteen   **Day Two**

If you grew up in a home like mine you were taught about actions and consequences. Every action has a consequence, some of them are good and some of them are not as pleasant. If you obeyed the rules and respected the family dynamics then the consequences were favorable. If you failed to hold up your family responsibilities then there was sure to be repercussions. Typical cause and effect is a law of nature and there is nothing we can do about it. We do not have to like it but we have to recognize that it does exist.

In God's economy we have the same limits placed on us. In the Old Testament Book of Isaiah 5:24, Isaiah is dealing with the disobedience of God's people. He tells them, "For they have rejected the law of the Lord of hosts and despised the Word of the Holy One of Israel." God does not just let inappropriate response to His commands just go by. He does not reward bad behavior nor does He believe that failure to know His ways are an excuse. God's Word is clear and His commands are available for all to know. We will be held responsible for our actions and there will be no excuses.

Reflections

Prayer

1 Chronicles 17:25
"For Thou, O my God, hast revealed to Thy servant that
Thou will build for him a house; therefore, Thy servant has
found courage to pray before Thee."

Week Fourteen   **Day Three**

Being polite was part of growing up in the Mayson family.
There was never any room for not showing common courtesy
to those around you. Yes, ma'am. Yes, sir. Please. Thank you.
All these were essential to a peaceful life in our home. Thank
you notes were a must as well. Every time we received a gift,
birthdays, Christmas or whatever, we made a note of who
gave it to us. We would then dispatch a thank you note to the
person who gave it to us.

I taught my son the same things when he was growing up.
It was amazing how many folks told me over the years what a
nice kid he was and so well behaved, all because he used his
manners. I do thank God for my son and for giving me the
wisdom to raise him in such a fashion.

David is praying here and thanking God for the promises
He has made to Him. Prayer is the perfect time to thank God
for what He has done for us. In David's case he is praying and
thanking God for what He is going to do for him. It is not all
about asking, prayers should be mostly about thanking God.
Prayer is a privilege and we must always remember that.

Reflections

Meditation

Joshua 23:8
"You are to cling to the Lord your God,
as you have done to this day."

Week Fourteen Day Four

The premise of my book, "When Life Shows Up," which is the companion volume to this devotional, is that stuff happens in life. You are either prepared or not. The best way to prepare is to develop spiritual disciplines that will strengthen your walk with God. Then when the stuff of life comes your way you will already be in shape to hear God's direction in the matter.

Joshua is giving his final instructions to God's people as they close out their efforts to inhabit the Promised Land. He basically says that you need to keep doing what got you here. Do not change things up after you go to your separate territories. You have made it this far by clinging to God. You have been discipling yourselves by meditating, listening to His guidance. Joshua says he will not be here much longer, you will have to do it on your own.

No since in reinventing the wheel. We know in good times we need to meditate, listen, journal on God's Word. Do not stop when life shows up, keep "clinging to the Lord your God."

Reflections

Physical Wellness

Galatians 2:20
"I have been crucified with Christ; and it is no longer I who
live but Christ lives in me…"

Week Fourteen   **Day Five**

As we grow older and begin to have families of our own, life's perspective changes. When we were young and single all we had to worry about is ourselves. We had certain freedoms that family folks did not have. We had only our needs to consider as we made decisions. The impact on others was limited when we were just one.

That dynamic changes as we start building a family. We put our needs and wants behind those whom we love-our wives, children, aging parents and even brothers and sisters in the faith. We seek the best for them and manage our self-care toward the end of our priorities.

Paul adds a new dimension to our thinking. He tells us that when we become Christians that it is not our life, it is God's life and He is living in us. What insight in our motivation to stay physically well, God is living in us. We are His host. We have His needs and direction to think about. We must stay prepared physically to accomplish His goals as His host.

Reflections

Fellowship

Acts 1:4
"Gathering them together, He commanded them to not leave Jerusalem, but wait for what the Father had promised…"

Week Fourteen   **Day Six**

What an exciting time for the followers of Christ. Jesus told His followers not to leave Jerusalem until this special event happened. He knew that once He ascended into heaven there would be a sense of loss and confusion. The folks who followed Him so faithfully would now not have His guidance and leadership.

We have all experienced these voids in our life. A role model, mentor, father or mother is no longer around to lean on. We are developing our spiritual strength but believe we still need to have someone around, just in case. Actually, if we are thinking these things then we are more mature in our faith than we give ourselves credit for.

Here Jesus tells the fellowship of believers to stay together. He wants them to comfort each other, lift each other up until this special event. No going alone. No quitting the team. No throwing in the towel and starting down another path.

The strength in the fellowship was necessary in those times. The numbers were few and each part of the group was needed to keep the whole as one. Stay strong in the fellowship, the miracle happens in the group.

Reflections

Service

Esther 4:14
"Who knows whether you have not attained royalty for such a time as this?"

Week Fourteen   **Day Seven**

I love this story. Queen Esther is in a struggle. Her cousin Mordecai is asking her to dig deep in her faith. A decree has gone out from the royal place that on a certain day that the ruling nation's people could kill any of the captive Jews they wanted. Esther and Mordecai were Jews and in a unique position to help their fellow countrymen.

Esther was the Queen and the favorite wife of the king. Mordecai is telling her to use her position to help her countrymen. A dangerous plea and one she knew could be life-threatening for her. Rightfully so, her cousin pointed out that it is just possible that the only reason she became queen was for this very lifesaving assignment.

The things God asks of us are rarely this dangerous and has not near the intrigue, but important in His plan. There are no small service opportunities in God's economy. Everything is necessary to accomplish His work on this earth. Look at your service opportunities as a way of being part of the greater salvation plan for this lost and dying world.

Reflections

Worship

John 4:23
"But an hour is coming, and now is, when the true worshipers shall worship the Father in spirit and truth; for such people the Father seeks to be His worshipers."

Week Fifteen   **Day One**

We find the story of the Samaritan woman at the well in John's gospel. Right after the discussions about all her husbands, she asks Jesus about worship (she's of the understanding that worship can only be done in Jerusalem). Jesus sets her straight. He tells her that "true worshipers" worship in spirit and truth. What does that even mean?

The word "worship" was originally spelled "worthship." Worthship means to be able to recognize the worth of the object worshipped. In other words, we have to know and understand God – through the other spiritual disciplines – to be able to worship. We need to know His might and truth and steadfastness and love. When we know these things, we can't help but worship Him!

Reflections

Bible Reading

Isaiah 51: 15, 16
"I am the Lord your God....
I have put my Words in your mouth."

Week Fifteen   **Day Two**

Part of the problems we have in life comes from believing that the world revolves around us. Yes, we think we are extremely unique and there is no one else with our particular skill sets or problems. Our needs and wants are more important and potentially linked to the survival of the planet. We have a need, actually a right to have everything we want so we can be satisfactorily in a position to keep the world turning. Does that sound right? I know I think that!

Sadly this very common thought is obviously not a correct one. If we would take the time to listen to others, we would find out we are all very similar and have plus and minuses in our life. Isaiah 51:15, 16 he tells us, "I am the Lord your God who stirs up the sea and the waves…I have put My words in your mouth…" Isaiah is telling us that God is in charge and His Words are what is important. He has placed them in our mouth and we need to be using them, not our own. The Bible is the source that aids us in knowing what these words are and when we need to be using them.

Reflections

Prayer

1 Thessalonians 5:18
"In everything give thanks;
for this is God's will for you in Christ Jesus."

Week Fifteen   **Day Three**

Prayer is also a time to thank God. We thank Him for answering prayers, we thank Him for his faithfulness, we thank Him for rain, financial stability, relationships, etc. Does that mean we have to thank God when things don't go our way or when we are in a jam? Paul says, however, that we are to give thanks for all circumstances.

I'm not saying this is an easy thing to do – or even one that comes naturally. For the Christian who really believes his prayers are heard and trusts God's wisdom and providence, everything should be a fulfillment of His will. Again, we don't always see the big picture and may not comprehend the Father's timing but, when all is said and done, what we truly want is to be a part of God's will. And when we are, we must thank the One that makes it happen.

Reflections

Meditation

Deuteronomy 32:46
"…Take to your heart all the words with which I am
warning you toady…"

Week Fifteen   **Day Four**

Deuteronomy 32 chronicles a song of Moses to the Israelites. He is encouraging his people to not only hear his words, but to retain them and reflect on them and, ultimately, apply them to their lives. This is what meditation is all about. It's simply not enough to just read our Bibles or listen to the teachings, but we need to really understand what God is saying to us and to keep them in our hearts so that they, instinctually, become a part of us, guiding our every thought and deed. When we do this, our hearts, minds, and souls become more Christ-like and it becomes obvious to those we come in contact with.

Reflections

Physical Wellness

Proverbs 3:7-8
"Be not wise in your own eyes; fear the Lord and turn away from evil. It will be healing to your flesh and refreshment to your bones."

Week Fifteen **Day Five**

I like that: "healing to your flesh and refreshment to your bones." That sounds quite lovely, doesn't it? It's true, though: when we are doing what we know to be right in the eyes of God, we always feel better, right? I mean, not always 100% but, for me, always better. Or more at peace. Or more content. Our physical wellbeing is so controlled by where our heads are. When we sin, our bodies are not healed and not refreshed; but when we turn towards God, maybe the aches and pains don't go away, but there is always a physical release.

Reflections

Fellowship

1 Corinthians 11:17
"In giving this instruction, I do not praise you, because you come together not for better, but for the worse."

Week Fifteen   **Day Six**

Paul is admonishing the Corinthians about how they had been approaching the Lord's supper. He tells them in verse 18, "...I hear that when you come together as a church, there are divisions among you..." Oops. How many times have you gone to church and felt like the outsider? How many times have you gone to church and you've not acknowledged or welcomed someone new?

Fellowship is not hanging out with your buddies, gossiping, and being oblivious to those around you. This is one of the biggest complaints I hear from people who don't like to go to church. In fact, I've been there. I've been in churches where it was the loneliest I felt all week long. Fellowship is about loving each other and having everyone feel a part of the body. Pay attention, open your eyes, include and love on a newbie.

Reflections

Service

Genesis 2:22
"The Lord God fashioned into a woman the rib which He had taken from the man and brought her to the man."

Week Fifteen   **Day Seven**

Why did God give Eve to Adam? I mean, was Eve made just for Adam's "enjoyment"? Yeah, I get all the companionship and sex and stuff. Adam didn't know he was missing out on all that. So why Eve?

God declares, "It is not good that man should be alone; I will make him a helper suitable for him" (v. 18). From the beginning of the human race, we were put on this earth – both men and women – to serve. Adam served God. Eve helped Adam. And so on. We were born to be of service to others as well as God.

As has been mentioned before (or will later), engaging in service is profoundly part of our make-up. When you give of yourself to someone else, when you put others before yourself, when you do something for somebody just because – you always, always, always feel amazing! That's because we are meeting a need our selves crave – and that simply feels good.

Reflections

Worship

Mathew 18:20
"For where two or more are gathered together in My name,
There I am in their midst."

Week Sixteen   **Day One**

When you are a little kid you want to have your freedom. You want to be a grown up, make decisions and do what you want. This is all part of growing up, of course. I was no different. I wanted a lot more freedom than I was allowed. Yet, it was always comforting knowing my parents were there. They had my back and even if I was restricted somewhat, I was comforted knowing they were around. This comfort I drew from the knowledge of their presence in my life allowed me to grow, to experiment and to move beyond their home.

The early church was new and needed direction. Jesus came when the religious leaders were oppressing the real worship of God with their multitude of rules. Jesus wanted theses chains broken and knew the early church would need encouragement after He was gone. It had to be comforting for them to know that God would be with them even if it was just a few of them gathered together. I take comfort in that as well; God is there always and for that He is worthy of my worship.

Reflections

Bible Reading

Deuteronomy 6:6
"And these words, which I am commanding you today,
shall be on your heart."

Week Sixteen   **Day Two**

Being human means that we tend to be fragile and need lots of attention. We tend to need to have lessons reinforced and constantly drilled into our heads. We do not always have to learn the hard way but we do need to have a certain amount of repetition in order to retain any knowledge that is worthwhile. It is just our nature, not necessarily some great defect that we all share. Anything worth doing is worth doing well and takes effort to keep the necessary facts in our minds.

Moses understood that the lessons God wanted us to learn had to be repeated and constantly thought about. These lessons had to be passed throughout the family and from one generation to another. In Deuteronomy 6:6, he tells us about God's Words, "These Words, which I am commanding you today, shall be on your heart..." Moses goes on to say we need to be teaching them constantly to those folks in our circle of influence. God's Words are so important they need to be a priority so we never forget them. Daily exposure to the Bible and other spiritual disciplines are necessary so that God's Word will remain in our hearts.

Reflections

Prayer

Psalms 145:18
"The Lord is near to all who call upon Him,
to all who call upon Him in truth."

Week Sixteen   **Day Three**

King David loved God and spent a lot of time singing His praises. We all know David started off his life as a shepherd boy living in Bethlehem. He ended up doing mighty things in the name of God. He became King of Israel, God's people. The Bible tells us he was a man after God's own heart.

Not all his life was glory and palace living. He had many obstacles to negotiate in life. Some of those were of his own making and some were part of God's personal development program. Even through all these growth opportunities David was still considered a man after God's own heart.

So, when he says that God is near to all who call Him, I believe it. I know David spent a lot of time in prayer, asking for guidance or even asking for forgiveness. David talked to God and allowed himself to be led by His Word. It worked for David, a man after God's own heart, and it will work for us.

Reflections

Meditation

Mathew 7:24
"Everyone who hears these words of Mine,
and act upon them, may be compared to the wise man,
who built his house upon the rock."

Week Sixteen   **Day Four**

There is nothing like having a great idea. You roll it over in your head. You look at it from different angles. You calculate the cost to implement this idea. Then the day comes and you leap into making the idea a reality. Low and behold the actualization of the idea turned out nothing like you wanted it to. Been there done that, and it is always humbling.

So, you learn from your mistakes and either try again or come up with another approach. It's a good learning development process. Trial, error and learn. On the other hand, when you keep doing the same thing and expecting different results, that is where you run into trouble. If nothing changes then nothing changes.

God wants us to be successful. He wants us to use His knowledge and wisdom to build our life on. If we do so then we will learn and grow through all the phases He leads us through. He considers us wise folks if we let Him lead.

Reflections

Physical Wellness

Revelation 12:6
"And the woman fled into the wilderness where she had a place prepared by God, so that she might be nourished…"

Week Sixteen   **Day Five**

I have always liked this passage. Yes, the Book of Revelation can be hard to understand, hard to get through. In fact, many folks I talk to never read it, too scary, too difficult to interpret. There are some eye-opening parts for sure but it is part of God's Word and we need to read it all.

This particular passage is where John is describing some of the future difficulties for the people who believe in God. There will be intense persecution of Christians by the powers that be, and difficult living like no one has ever seen before. There will be war on earth and war in heaven as human history comes to a close, it will be chaotic. It will be a time beyond all humans' ability to endure.

With all this chaos, John is telling us that God will provide a place of refuge. A place that He has prepared because He knew it would be needed. A place where those gathered can be nourished. A place where God will be to care for His children.

I draw great comfort that God is doing that now for us. I want to do my part to ensure my mind, spirit and body are prepared to meet the challenges that lay ahead. Nothing like the end times are here yet but there are many challenges to be met, I want to be ready.

Reflections

Fellowship

Daniel 2:17,18
"Daniel went to his house and informed his friends…
in order that they might request compassion from the God
of heaven concerning this mystery…"

Week Sixteen   **Day Six**

I grew up in a military household and then was in the military myself. I understand moving. Moving myself, helping others move, it's one of my superpowers. I have done it by myself and I have had help from others. It's always a lot easier when you have help.

Problems are the same way. They say a problem shared is a problem halved. If you can learn to ask for help, whether it is for moving or problem solving, the task is easier. There is no shame in asking for help. In fact, that is one way God spreads His blessings around by us helping each other.

Daniel and his friends have their backs against the wall. Unless they could interpret the king's dream, they would be killed. As a group, a fellowship of believers, they prayed. Daniel did not go to his prayer closet alone; he asked his friends for help. He knew this was a mighty task and he would need the fellowship's strength to accomplish it.

Do not be quick to do the "lone ranger" thing. Allow yourself the blessing of help from others. When you do so they get a blessing as well. The strength is in the fellowship.

Reflections

Service

Hebrews 12:28
"Let us show gratitude, by which we may offer to God an
acceptable service with reverence and awe."

Week Sixteen   **Day Seven**

You cannot hit a baseball from the bench or in the dugout or without a bat. You must be at the plate, correctly positioned with a bat. Now it still may be difficult to hit a fast ball or a curve. Nevertheless, you are now in position to be successful.

Success comes when preparation and opportunity meet. We can do little about the opportunity but we can get prepared. I do not know if I will get in the baseball game or if I will get a chance to bat. I can, however, practice batting so when the opportunity arises, I have a chance to get a hit.

We need to be of service to others. It is a way God blesses people. He uses those who can help and positions them to help those who are in need. We will never be called into service if we do not first understand gratitude. We will only be blessed if we serve and we cannot serve unless we become grateful. You cannot hit without a bat and you cannot serve without gratitude. If you want to be of service you must learn to be grateful.

Reflections

Worship

Matthew 19:26
"With people this is impossible,
but with God all things are possible."

Week Seventeen   **Day One**

Webster's dictionary defines "worship" as to show reverence or to regard with extravagant respect. The *intransitive* verb means to take part in an act of worship. Yes, worship is a noun, but it is definitively a verb. As we all recall from our elementary grammar lessons, a verb means action. Action means getting off our butts and actually doing something.

Do we regard God with extravagant respect? What does that even mean? Perhaps it means that we put everything – in order of importance in our lives - behind God. Perhaps it means that we submerge ourselves in His Word. Perhaps it means we live our lives as Christ lived His. Perhaps it means all three. The take-away from today's reflection is that worship is action; it is something that we *do*. Take a moment and really meditate on what worship looks like in your life.

Reflections

Bible Reading

Joshua 23:14

"Now behold, today I am going the way of all the earth, and you know in all your hearts and in all your souls that not one word of all the good words which the Lord your God spoke concerning you has failed; all have been fulfilled for you, not one of them has failed."

Week Seventeen   **Day Two**

Today there are a lot of false claims, promises and information being provided as answers to our needs. There is an application for every need available on our "smart phone" or a pill that we can take to solve all our physical and mental problems. We see things advertised on TV that claim to be able to meet all our needs ranging from getting rid of squirrels, low car insurance or help with psychic connections. All of them claim to be honest, true and dependable.

We have all bought into these false claims and have the frustrations to go along with it. The truth is that everything produced by man is questionable in its ability to solve our problems. Some may be good for the masses but are of no help to those who fall into areas of exception. In Joshua 23:14, he reminds the people of God that, "Not one word of all the good words which the Lord your God spoke concerning you has failed…" It is good to know that there is a source of truth that can be trusted and that will never fail you. People are people and will eventually fail you, but God's Word never will. Something you can count on always is unique and a wonderful source of strength.

Reflections

Prayer

Jonah 1:14
"They called on the Lord and said, 'We earnestly pray,
O Lord, do not let us perish…'"

Week Seventeen   **Day Three**

I don't remember exactly when it was during Charlie's hideous foray through Virginia's legal system, but I do remember it was on the eve of some important decision the court was due to hand out. We were talking on the phone and he shared with me that he had been praying "like when you do as a child, squeezing your eyes shut, tensing your whole body and begging God." I suspect that would be the definition of earnestly praying - where every cell of your being is facing the Almighty, pleading and beseeching His mercy.

Sometimes our prayers are merely a passing thought. Other times we find ourselves – our entire selves – intensely bargaining or begging God. Even though God doesn't always answer our prayers the way we would like – and this was true in Charlie's case – God does hear us. And I believe His heart breaks for us when He has to answer the prayer differently from what we want. As hard as this is to comprehend oftentimes, everything God does is for good.

Reflections

Meditation

Matthew 22:8
"The wedding is ready,
but those who were invited were not worthy."

Week Seventeen   **Day Four**

Charlie maintains in his book, *When Life Shows Up*, that meditation as a spiritual discipline is "probably the most important one we can master" (p. 161). He refers to meditation as "listening." Listening, according to Charlie, involves 1) us being cognizant to the Word coming into our heads; 2) processing it; and 3) acting upon that processed Word.

Yep – action. Webster's defines action as "a thing done." Boom. This means that when we meditate, most often there will be something (we like to call it a duty assignment) that is expected of us. That's what meditation is all about. Listening to God for direction in our lives!! How many times have you longed to "hear from God"? Meditate.

Reflections

Physical Wellness

Philippians 3:21
"who will transform the body of our humble state into
conformity with the body of His glory...."

Week Seventeen   **Day Five**

This scripture talks about God releasing us - with unlimited power - from our earthly bodies and replacing it with our heavenly bodies. Which means no pain, no imperfections, no missing limbs or body parts, no cellulite! I truly look forward to that day!!

Even though we get new, perfect "bodies" after we die, we are still responsible for taking care of our human ones as best we can. That will mean specific differences for each of us but, overall, I think we know the importance of exercise, diet, good mental and physical health. I also understand that these aren't necessarily easy for any of us. We all struggle somehow when it comes to physical wellness. You're not alone, but what sets us apart from others is that we know who our bodies house – the Holy Spirit!

Reflections

Fellowship

Proverbs 13:20
"He who walks with wise men will be wise, but the
companion of fools will suffer harm."

Week Seventeen   **Day Six**

In other words, "you're the company you keep." Solomon's words to the wise, if you will, triggers the "duh" response, but how many times have I surrounded myself with "fools" and it turned out well? Uh, zero – unless you count the fact that after many, many fools and many, many heartaches, I started to become wiser and more discerning. And I don't know that it gets easier, either.

As important as fellowship is, *who* we fellowship with is as important. I try to surround myself with strong women who are confident enough and love me enough to call me on my stuff. I need that. I surround myself with Christians – the real kind who make the hard choices and are consistent in their lives and faith. These are people who are going to help me grow - as a woman and as a Christian – and become who God needs me to be!

Reflections

Service

Matthew 10:42
"And whoever in the name of a disciple gives to one of these little ones even a cup of cold water to drink, truly I say to you, he shall not lose his reward."

Week Seventeen   **Day Seven**

Throughout this devotional Charlie and I have and will suggest different types of service work. It is important, I believe, that we each volunteer our time and gifts on a regular basis. This helps service become second-nature to us and lets others count on us.

This verse, however, emphasizes the little things. See, these opportunities, as small and insignificant as they may seem, are used by God to make differences in others' lives – and sometimes huge differences! I'm talking about holding the door open for someone, paying for the meal of the guy behind you at a fast-food joint, smiling at a stranger, asking someone how they are and really be interested in their answer, picking up a piece of trash, giving that harried mom a look of "you're doing a great job!" These are all little things – but you still get points and if you do it enough, it will start to define the person you're becoming – Christ-like!

Reflections

Worship

Revelation 15:8
"The temple was filled with smoke from the glory of God and from His power..."

Week Eighteen   **Day One**

If you have ever gone to a major sporting event there is a lot of hype before the contest begins. No matter what sport, there is a big to-do made to build the contest up. Sometimes there are fireworks, smoke fills the arena, fog machines are used so teams can run through it. It is fun to be there, so much excitement and anticipation run through the crowd. Energy flows through the crowd trying to fuel their team. It's a great experience!

As Christians we believe that God created everything that is. We believe He has always maintained control of our world and everything that is in it. We also believe at an appointed time He will have control of the closing out of human history.

In today's scripture we praise God because He is closing out human history. Smoke fills the temple; the seven plagues are finished and now the bowls of judgment will begin. It is a grand scene. It is an exciting time in heaven and for the participants. God has a plan; it is working and we will be the benefactors in time. Praise God!

Reflections

Bible Reading

2 Chronicles 6:17
"O Lord the God of Israel, let Thy word be confirmed which Thou hast spoken to Thy servant David."

Week Eighteen   **Day Two**

All of us have had to deal with broken promises. Not just the ones that are innocently forgotten about or unintentionally overlooked. It is those promises that are tendered with malice-of-forethought that really takes the wind out of our sails. We look forward and even trust that a certain word will be kept and are devastated at the realization that we are standing out in the cold. What makes broken promises even more devastating is when they come from those we expect better from. It is like having a rug jerked out from underneath you or the air blasted from your lungs.

   After King Solomon takes the throne from his father King David he prays to God. In 2 Chronicles 6:17, Solomon asks God to "Let Thy word be confirmed which Thou hast spoken to Thy servant David." King Solomon is counting on God's promises to his father King David to be kept. He knows he has a role to play in the covenant agreement but realizes that it is God's promises that are important. We can trust God's Word to be good for us now and forever.

Reflections

Prayer

Joel 3:10
"Beat your plow shears into swords, your pruning hooks into spears; let the weak say, I am a mighty man…"

Week Eighteen   **Day Three**

Joel is one of those prophets who sole job was to warn God's people of upcoming punishment. God had given His people all the chances they were going to get. He sent Joel out to let them know to get ready. Gracious of God to forewarn His people that He is fed up with their disobedience.

Life brings us curve balls all the time. The premise of the companion book to this devotional is just that. Life will show up and the best way to handle it is to get ready. Lifestyle changes need to be made so that preparation - spiritually, physically and mentally - can be made.

Joel is telling the listeners that they need to make weapons. They need to psyche themselves up by saying they are strong and ready. The weak need to be believing they are strong, punishment is coming.

We have to do the same thing in life. We have the privilege of prayer as a tool as well. We can go to God first and seek guidance, strength and comfort. Prayer, a very underutilized privilege.

Reflections

Meditation

Hebrews 10:23
"Let us hold fast the confession of our hope without wavering, for He who promised is faithful…"

Week Eighteen   **Day Four**

There is nothing worse than giving up just before the miracle happens in your life. You wait, hope and pray for God to provide for your needs. Something big is on the horizon, life and death at times. You rely on God and then when you cannot take it any more you follow your own plan. Use your own strength. Rely on your own wisdom. Sound familiar?

The human condition is geared to self-reliance. Even as we seek to develop spiritual disciplines, we still fall back to our default position at times, reliance on self. We cannot help it; we are humans and the world beats into our heads that self is the ruler. We do have all the elements internally required for success.

Today, the writer of Hebrews is telling us to hold on. Through our meditation with God we can hold fast to the truths we know about Him. He loves us and is in control. He will provide and His timing is always perfect. Keep the faith friends, do not give up before God shows you His love, practically in your life.

Reflections

Physical Wellness

Psalms 16:5
"The Lord is the portion of my inheritance and my cup;
Thou dost support my lot."

Week Eighteen   **Day Five**

God has a plan for us. He wants us to be part of His ministry on earth. He can see what we need to do tomorrow, so He is preparing us today. Nothing gets done in His economy by accident, no coincidences in His plan. He knows, He does and He is always successful.

In King David's short song, he is praising God for all that he has received. He is describing the beauty of his life and what God has given him. David knows where his strength comes from and who is responsible for all that happens around him.

We need to do our part. We need to keep ourselves prepared for service to God. Our bodies need to move into action when called. Like an athlete who comes off the bench, he needs to be ready at all times. He never knows when he will be called to perform in a way he has been training. We get all from God, our portions are given by Him, our cups are filled by Him, we must be prepared to serve Him at all times.

Reflections

Fellowship

Exodus 2:24, 25
"So, God heard their groaning; and God remembered His
covenant…and God saw the sons of Israel,
and God took notice of them."

Week Eighteen   **Day Six**

Today we are out in the desert with Moses. He is tending his flock like he has been doing the last forty years. His first forty years he was raised in Egypt with a silver spoon in his mouth. The last forty years were not like the first. Now the next forty years will be a complete change as well.

God knows where we are, what is going on with us and what is happening around us. We are His people and He cares. He cares about us as individual sheep of His pasture and He cares for the flock. The flock, the fellowship, the group is important. We gather together as like-minded participants in this journey called life. We are important to each other.

God heard the groaning of His people, captive in Egypt. We as individuals are heard by God. Wonder how much more volume the fellowship has, how much more attention the heavens give us as we groan to God collectively. God knows all and has life under control. There is a special premium put on our fellowship when we act in unison, for a common purpose and even when we suffer together. Join the group!

Reflections

Service

Mathew 10:16
"Behold, I send you out as sheep in the midst of wolves;
therefore, be shrewd as serpents, and innocent as doves."

Week Eighteen   **Day Seven**

Welders weld. Fishermen fish. Taxi drivers transport. Christians evangelize. It's pretty easy to see that we do what we are trained to do. It's not a big mystery. It seems so simple but so often things get messed up. Why go to a plumber to get your taxes done? Why go to the florist for a root canal?

God has given us all desires that leads to utilizing the gifts He gives us. Sure, they must be developed and we must learn how to use them for His purpose. They are all important and they all are part of His master plan.

Yet, so often we set out to do someone else's job. We set out to get our needs met by someone who is not qualified to meet them. We fall for schemes of the world that says one size fits all, everyone's needs can be met in one place by one person.

Jesus prepared these folks to do the job of the evangelist. He gave them instructions on what to do, how to do and how to react to push back from the dissenters. Notice these servants did not go out and do the work of a doctor, or farmer, or tent maker. They served in the capacity in which they had been trained.

Not everything the world wants can I provide. Even if I wanted to, I cannot. God has given me gifts and I am only effective when I am using them. Others are gifted differently; they fulfill other needs in God's plan. I have to stay in my own lane, do as I have been gifted and leave the other areas to those who know better.

Reflections

Worship

John 3:16
"For God so loved the world, that He gave His only
begotten Son..."

Week Nineteen   **Day One**

This is God's Gospel in a holy nutshell. And it's everywhere: on billboards, placards at the ballgame, bumper stickers – everywhere. It tells us that our God loved us – all of us, by the way – so much that He allowed the earthly life of His only Son, Jesus, to be surrendered as payment for the rest of us and our sins. What do the rest of us get? Eternal life. With God. And Jesus. And the Holy Spirit. Pretty sweet deal, isn't it?

This *is* a worship song if ever there was one! Let that sink in: someone loves you so much that they are willing to give up a most important entity to spend forever with you. Pretty heady stuff. Stop right now, close your eyes (well, after you finished reading), say these words out loud and feel the truth of these words and let the impact of this statement wash over you.

Reflections

Bible Reading

Deuteronomy 5:5
"I was standing between the Lord and you at the time to
declare to you the Word of the Lord..."

Week Nineteen   **Day Two**

When I was a child, I was blessed to have parents who stood
between me and the world. They took the responsibility of
shielding me from the dangers of the "big bad" world. My
parents, at times, even had to step in and protect me from
"me," when my youth and immaturity got me into situations
I had no clue how to resolve. That was their job they declared
and my parents took it seriously. Like it or not they placed
themselves between me and the potential for harm as long as
I was under their roof.

Moses found himself in the same situation many times
when he was dealing with God's people as he led them toward
the Promised Land. In Deuteronomy 5:5 we find Moses
repeating the Ten Commands to a new generation saying in
preparation, "I was standing between the Lord and you at a
time..." Moses tells them that he did this so he could "declare
the Word of the Lord..." Moses knew that it was obedience
to God's Word that would ultimately determine if they were
successful in the new land. Today it is the same, adherence to
God's Word is the only way to continue in the correct posture
before Him.

Reflections

Prayer

Hosea 14:2

"Take words with you and return to the Lord. Say to Him, 'Take away all inequity and receive us graciously, that we may present the fruit of our lips'."

Week Nineteen   **Day Three**

God wants to hear from us. He wants to hear our voice. He wants to hear our sadness, our happiness, our concerns, our hopes, our wants. But when we first come to Him, we must come in a position of repentance. The very nature of God is such that He cannot be around sin and, as basically sinful creatures that we are, we almost always come to him covered in sin. So, we must repent first.

And it really needs to be sincere. Just throwing out a "Forgive me" and think it covers everything is certainly not the way it's done. We must dig deep, sometimes, and really look at our thoughts and behaviors in order to be sincere about asking for His forgiveness. Until then, God is unable to hear the rest of what's in our hearts.

Reflections

Meditation

1 Corinthians 13:11
"When I was a child, I used to speak like a child, think like a child, reason like a child; when I became a man, I did away with childish things."

Week Nineteen   **Day Four**

Today's Scripture dovetails with yesterday's in that as we grow as Christians, our words, thoughts, and deeds grow as well. When we make meditation a daily part of who we are, our thoughts deepen and mature. We tend to think of others instead of ourselves. We start to see situations in a light that shows us the whole picture – not just spotlighting us.

Meditation gives us the chance to really reflect on ourselves and as we develop and strengthen our relationship with the Holy Spirit, we are able to understand things in a more Christ-like way. Like anything, though, meditation takes training and time....and growth.

Reflections

Physical Wellness

Matthew 6:16
"Whenever you fast, do not put on a gloomy face..."

Week Nineteen   **Day Five**

One of my favorite gripes about us Christians is our preponderance for playing the martyr. "Oh, I've given up [fill in the blank] for Lent. It's such a struggle. Poor me." The same goes for fasting (or anything we're doing for the Lord). Fasting is all about denying our physical needs in order to cleanse our souls so that we can focus on God. What a wonderful place to be – in the presence of the Holy Spirit. And yet, we mess that up by complaining about it.

The second part of this is what we look like to non-believers. Who in the world would sign up to follow Christ if those of us who already do act like it is such a pain? We should be thrilled. We should consider it an honor to be in a place that God can meet with us and talk with us and enhance our spirituality.

Reflections

Fellowship

Genesis 2:20b
"For Adam there was not found a helper suitable for him…"

Week Nineteen   **Day Six**

Apparently, all the bugs and birds and animals were not fulfilling Adam's need for companionship and partnership. I get that. So, God provided someone for Adam to fellowship with. That's how important fellowship is. Yes, Eve served other positions as helpmate, but being able to listen and communicate and empathize and understand Adam is what he really needed.

It's what we all really need. That is why fellowship is so important. And to fellowship with other Christians helps us to focus in on what is truly important. Just as Eve certainly helped Adam in so many different ways, our time with others in fellowship offers growth in our relationship with God.

Reflections

Service

Mark 2:17
"It is not those who are healthy who need a physician,
but those who are sick."

Week Nineteen   **Day Seven**

Jesus did not come to heal righteous people, but rather sinful ones. Think about it: most of the stories about Jesus show him attending to those in need. Of course, His end game was to introduce Himself, God, and eternal life, but to get there He spent His time with "the sick".

So should we. When we are out and about, our focus should be on those who are in need – both physically and spiritually. To "get our foot in the door," being of service to those who don't know Jesus is the best way to actually show the non-believer what Jesus is/was all about.

Reflections

Worship

Deuteronomy 6:13
"You shall fear only the Lord your God; and you shall
worship Him and swear by His name."

Week Twenty   **Day One**

Rules are rules. You cannot live in society without them. Most of us understand that and live within the societal norms. It's pretty easy for us because we were taught from an early age there are consequences for our actions. Those consequences can either be good or bad depending on our actions. Every action does have a consequence - easy, right?

Guess not! Look at all the laws we have enacted in this country. One thing I have learned about rules is that they come about because someone has violated normal human common sense. Someone always tries to infringe their wants or greed for their own good and has hurt someone else in the process. So a rule or law has to be enacted as a result.

Moses is telling the children of God, as they begin to invade the Promised Land, that they only are to worship God. It makes sense to me; however, why does He have to say that? Because now their default tendency will be to worship the gods of the people whose land they are entering. God must insist we worship only Him. There are no gray areas in this commandment. We wonder why our life is not moving forward spiritually, what are we worshipping should be a question we ask ourselves.

Reflections

Bible Reading

Matthew 6:33
"But seek first His kingdom and His righteousness; and all
these things shall be added to you."

Week Twenty   **Day Two**

As I look to move forward in my Christian life there seems to
be so many decisions to make. I try to be a good father, son,
husband, preacher and friend. I want to be the example I need
to be for God and I do not want to be so rigid that I scare folks
away from the loving God I know. So as a result there is a daily
struggle to balance my faith with my practical interaction with
my fellow man. The problem I face is when "to do" something
and when "not to do" something else!

The good news for me is that the Bible has an answer for
folks who find themselves bogged down with life's decisions.
In the Gospel of Matthew 6:33, Jesus tells us to "Seek first
His kingdom and His righteousness and all these things will
be added to you." That is the answer; seek what God wants
and He will sort out the earthly things that need to be done.
Being in God's Word is the way to seek God's plan, nowhere
else. We do not go to the store and buy it; we cannot order it
online nor can we pick it up at a flea market.

Reflections

Prayer

Daniel 2:17, 18
"So, Daniel went to his house and informed his friends…in order that they might request compassion from the God of heaven concerning this mystery…"

I was at a Bible study earlier this week at a friend's church out of town. I did not know anyone there except my friend and his wife. We had a time of prayer before the study started and it was sparsely attended. The Bible study, however, was very well attended. We talked about this on the way home.

I certainly need to continue to work on my prayer life. I know that it has to be an intentional effort. It's funny how Christians underutilize prayer, especially before beginning a time of Bible study. Then we wonder why we do not get understanding or growth from it.

Daniel was never like that. He had a constant daily routine of prayer. In this case he had a special "mystery" to solve. The first thing he did was pray about it. No hovering around a coffee pot, burning the midnight oil trying to come up with the solution. Prayer is always the first part of the solution. Then for Daniel, and now for us.

Reflections

Meditation

2 Corinthians 5:7
"We walk by faith, not by sight…also we have as our
ambition, whether at home or absent,
to be pleasing to Him."

Week Twenty   **Day Four**

In my first church there was this little old lady who was there every time the doors opened. She did not have a key, so many times I would drive up to open the church and she would be waiting on the front porch. She did not drive so she would walk the mile from her house, with her dog, to the church. No matter what the weather was like she would be there and seems like always before me.

We got to talking about her devotion to God and this little rural church. She would paraphrase this verse and tell me the Bible says to "walk" by faith. She wanted to be pleasing to God and she knew being gathered with the fellowship of believers pleased Him.

When I would visit her in her trailer it seemed I always came during her meditation time. How could that be, I wondered, that every time I showed up, she "happened" to be meditating. The answer was that she was always meditating. She believed God's Word and took it seriously. She lived a simple life. Her early years were rough and misfortune seemed to plague her. Nevertheless, during this phase of her life there was peace and contentment. Wonder why?

Reflections

Physical Wellness

Amos 7:14
"I am not a prophet nor am I the son of a prophet;
for I am a herdsman and a grower of sycamore figs."

Week Twenty   **Day Five**

I read a statistic years ago that the average man changes careers three times in his lifetime. They listed several different reasons for the change. The main one seemed to be because of the economy and the ability for the current career to support the man and his family.

The article went on to point out that often these moves were into areas that were completely different than what they had been doing before. I can verify the one fact in my life. Every time I made a move it was into a completely different area than before.

In today's passage God has asked Amos to do something completely different than what he was used to doing. Many other heroes of the faith outlined in the Bible were asked to do the same thing. The first question that comes to my mind when I read about these changes is their readiness to do their new job. How fit were they to endure these new challenges.

I often wonder if folks do not get new, more involved assignments from God because they are not physically able to take the strain. God is trying to prepare me today for my job tomorrow. If I do not allow Him to do so by being disobedient, will I get the job? How many folks are dissatisfied or feel underused because they are not fit for their next task?

Reflections

Fellowship

Galatians 1:15,16
"…He who had set me apart…was pleased to reveal His Son
in me, that I might preach Him among the Gentiles, I did
not immediately consult with flesh and blood."

Week Twenty   **Day Six**

As a member of a Twelve Step Group, there is an emphasis
on the fellowship. I need the fellowship to help me learn how
to overcome my problem with addiction. My best thinking
got me to a place where the addiction was ruining my life. I
needed some other inputs to change the way I thought. The
group did that for me.

After saying this, there were times when I needed to do
for myself. I had to read the "Big Book," do some personal
inventory work and make amends. All this was done on my
own. I had to put individual effort into my recovery.

Paul is talking about his own recovery. His own journey
from persecuting the new church to being one of its pillars.
He had contact with folks who could lead and guide him but
there was some alone time that was needed. The fellowship
available was necessary. Ultimately, his individual efforts to
grow spiritually was a must.

As we study to improve our spiritual walk, spiritual
disciplines are a must. We have to keep in balance our personal
instruction time with God and the practical application of our
calling within the fellowship.

Reflections

Service

Proverbs 16:7
"When a man's ways are pleasing to the Lord, he makes even his enemies to be at peace with him."

Week Twenty   **Day Seven**

My Dad told me once, actually many times, that not everybody is going to like me. The first time he told me that was when I was a senior in high school. There was a kid on the soccer team that did not like me because my Dad was a commissioned officer and his was a non-commissioned officer (NCO). What?

I wanted to get along with everyone. Until that point in my young life, to my knowledge, I was well liked and had no known enemies. As an adult I have always been in management positions. I often had folks who were displeased with me, my decisions or just my looks.

By the time I became a Pastor I knew that I would not please everyone. I absolutely could not. What I could do in my efforts to serve my congregation and the community was follow the advice of this wise proverb. My job was to follow God's Word; being obedient means treating folks the way God wanted me to. I was able to serve some of the mean folks, mostly church folks, using this advice. I wanted to serve and knew that all folks needed to know God's love in a practical way. I vouch for the wisdom of this proverb.

Reflections

Worship

Deuteronomy 6:14
"You shall not follow other gods, any of the gods of the peoples who surround you."

Week Twenty-One   **Day One**

We truly must be mindful of what we worship! When we talk about "any of the gods" of the people around us, this doesn't just mean some ugly metal image someone built to pray to, but it includes all the other things we tend to put before God in this day and age. Money, relationships, drugs, sex, power, prestige, food...you get the idea.

If we put anything before God, that becomes our god – little "g". Plain and simple. But if we spend time every day studying, meditating, acting on God's Word, we worship Him and He builds a hedge of protection around us to keep all those other gods at bay.

Reflections

Bible Reading

John 1:1a
"In the beginning, there was the Word…"

Week Twenty-One   **Day Two**

It is wonderful living in the age of such advanced technology. Having so much information available at your fingertips can really make life much more manageable. Of course too much of anything is never good but if, as individuals, we limit our dependence on technology then we will not suffer as much when, for whatever reason, we do not have it. I have a friend whose son could not change the channel on the TV, because he misplaced the remote. I guess getting off the couch and manually pushing the channel button did not occur to this lad. As technology advances, our societies' norms and priorities change as well. Since the technology changes so fast we are often left with this whirlwind disruption of what *is* and is *not* available for our edification.

Change is good; yet, if it leads us away from basic principles that guide our life then we are left with a void that can be filled by not so desirable standards. The Bible lets us know that God will always be the same and will not change with the times. In the Gospel of John 1:1, the disciple tells us that "In the beginning was the Word…" That same Word is with us now and will be with us until the close of human history. No changes, no faulty glitches or necessary upgrades. The Word of God will transcend time and always be applicable to us on any date.

Reflections

Prayer

Ezekiel 34:11
"Behold, I Myself will search for
My sheep and seek them out."

Week Twenty-One   **Day Three**

Do you ever wonder what to pray? Or how to pray? Sometimes, prayer comes easily to me. Other days, it seems illusive. We're not alone. Jesus' crew – the disciples – made the same request, "Lord, teach us to pray" (Luke 11:1). Sometimes we seek God out. Other times, He seeks us. We are likened, quite often in the Bible, as sheep and God as the shepherd. The Bible makes it clear that every sheep is important to Him and He will seek out those that stray and bring them back to the flock.

When you're struggling with prayer, take comfort in that God will seek you out. Thank Him. And listen.

Reflections

Meditation

Galatians 1:10
"For am I now seeking the favor of men, or of God?"

Week Twenty-One   **Day Four**

This is a good foundation of our meditation...are we meditating on God? Or other people and things? Meditation doesn't "work" if we aren't meditating on the right things and in the right spirit. Here, Paul is commenting on how his relationship with God comes first and that it is far more important to consider what God thinks.

It is easy for us to get caught up in what other people think. We're human; it's part of our sinful nature. However, our whole relationship with God has absolutely nothing to do with anyone else – it is an incredibly intimate relationship with no room for any distractions. When we meditate, let's focus on that relationship.

Reflections

Physical Wellness

Jonah 4:6
"So the Lord God appointed a plant and it grew up over
Jonah to be a shade over his head to deliver him from his
discomfort. And Jonah was extremely happy about the plant."

Week Twenty-One   **Day Five**

In our daily lives, I think we miss way too many "gifts" and
"answers to unspoken prayers". In this passage, Jonah is sitting
in the scorching sun – and is miserable. Jonah didn't ask God
to produce a plant that would shade him, but He did. And
that plant did, indeed, give Jonah the respite from the heat and
"his discomfort". And then Jonah did it – he acknowledged
the shade and it completely changed his mood and outlook.

Oftentimes, our physical comforts – or discomforts –
actually do alter the way we feel. There have been many times
where I have been working outside, sweating to death and, out
of nowhere, a cool breeze comes by! I didn't ask God for the
breeze – He just knew that I was uncomfortable and He knew
exactly what would change that. These are the times that we
need to be oh so aware of and grateful for. This is God talking
to us and showing His amazing love for us.

Reflections

Fellowship

James 1:19
"…But everyone must be quick to hear,
slow to speak and slow to anger."

Week Twenty-One   **Day Six**

Fellowship is about serving God and James tells us exactly how to do that. Listening is not an easy task. To really hear what a person is saying to us, we must truly listen to that person. All too often we find ourselves only half-listening to a person, waiting for our turn to talk. One of the greatest acts of kindness and fellowship is to really pay attention and listen to what another person is saying. We need to listen from a place of love.

The second part of this passage is sound advice: be slow to speak and slow to anger. When we are doing all the talking, we learn nothing. We just become output-only devices! Without input, we stay stagnant. Oftentimes we find ourselves only half-hearing what someone is saying, filling in the blanks with our own perceptions and thoughts, and find that we are annoyed or angry at the speaker. Let's try, today, to actually listen to others.

Reflections

Service

Ecclesiastes 4:9
"Two are better than one because they have a good return
for their labor."

Week Twenty-One   **Day Seven**

Not only does God tell us to do service work, but He also
tells us how to do it. Solomon talks about the emptiness a
person can have who keeps to themselves, not interacting with
others. We are social creatures. Even those of us who tend
to be more introverted still need companionship. There is
something wonderful about doing service work with other
people. Have you ever noticed it? Folks will get together to, say,
prepare meals for the homeless and find unexpected payoffs.
Solomon is correct when he says that more working together
can get more done, but there is also the added benefit of being
with others in the service of God. So often, after completing a
service work, I feel that I was impacted more than the people
on the receiving end.

Reflections

Worship

"Be on guard for yourselves and for all the flock, among which the Holy Spirit has made you overseers, to shepherd the church of God, which He purchased with His own blood."

Week Twenty-Two   **Day One**

There is a saying, "If you do not stand for something, you will fall for anything." What a true statement. The most dangerous people in the world are those who do not stand for anything; no moral compass to guide them, no concept of a Higher Power that directs their spiritual concepts, no belief in anything but themselves with total disregard for those around them.

Say what you want about organized religion, but it is important. There has to be a system that helps provide a template or model for our belief. Not just anything is helpful to believe. Religion provides those who believe with a set of standard interpretations for their beliefs.

Luke is telling us this very same thing. He writes to the Gentiles about guarding themselves against those who have no real interest in their spiritual growth but to tear it down. The Holy Spirit will enable us to know how to interpret God's Word. We are all overseers and shepherds of the correct rendering of God's Word, God's plan for us as believers. We worship God because He has provided for us and will continue to lead us toward Himself. Take this seriously and praise God for His care and protection today.

Reflections

Bible Reading

John 8:31
"If you abide in My Word,
then you are truly disciples of Mine…"

Week Twenty-Two   **Day Two**

I guess that I dislike rules as much as anyone else. Maybe I just have a problem with authority or think that rules are for the weak and undisciplined. The problem with that attitude is that most rules serve a purpose and help humans all stay on the same sheet of music. If no one stopped for red lights then traveling by automobile would always be dangerous. If drinking and driving were legal then, again, automobile transit would be a challenge. Rules work for the betterment of the whole, the group is benefited.

I can walk around in violation of this world's laws and receive certain reparations but to start violating God's rules, different story. God does not fine, give probation or accept excuses. In John 8:31, Jesus tells us that "If you abide in My Word, then you are truly disciples of mine." This gives us the implied converse; if you do not "abide" then you are not disciples of God. There is no gray area there, just fact. You obey and you are considered disciples, if you do not then you are not. The Bible is God's Word and makes His commandments clear to us. We have no excuse for disobedience or creating gray areas to live in.

Reflections

Prayer

Jeremiah 42:2
"Please let our petition come before you,
pray for us to the Lord your God…"

Week Twenty-Two   **Day Three**

Most of my life I have been one of those people who would rather ask forgiveness than for permission. Being a self-proclaimed know-it-all, I would rather do things my way than worry about others' input. As a rule, that philosophy streamlined my progress towards a certain goal. It was, however, not a reliable process in actually being successful.

As I write about spiritual disciplines, I must say that beginning something new is not easy, just like breaking old habits. The good news for me is when I began to develop the discipline to pray for answers and guidance, my success rate increased. I still get in my own way at times but when I allow God to lead, guide and direct me I am always at peace during the process.

Jeremiah is being asked if God would approve their plan to migrate to Egypt. I'm not going to go through all the history but God tells Jeremiah no. God was petitioned, asked for His direction. What we do with that is our own choice. We need to get in the habit of doing this. It will save us a lot of heartache and stress.

Reflections

Meditation

Ephesians 1:9
"He made known to us the mysteries of His will, according
to His kind intention which He purposed in Him…"

Week Twenty-Two   **Day Four**

The act of meditation was kind of confusing to me. I thought I had to sit somewhere with my legs crossed, hands on my knees with my thumb and forefinger making an "O". I thought I had to be chanting or humming something that was supposed to clear my mind. This, in fact, can be a way to do it. Or you can just wait on God.

There are no real guidelines to do so. If you can hear God while fishing, then do that. If working in the yard clears your mind, do that. I like being on my Harley motorcycle, with the wind in my face, relaxing to the roar of my engine. Whatever works to put you in a posture to listen will work.

Paul is telling those believers in his letter to the Ephesians that God will make known to them the things they need to know. He will provide for them what is necessary to move forward in their spiritual journey. Paul does not mandate some posture, time or ritualistic need to hear these instructions.

God wants to communicate with us. He often does so at times you least expect. Waiting for His Word is necessary. Being alert for them is important as well. He is not trying to make it difficult or demanding certain hoops to be jumped through. Like anything else, practice makes perfect.

Reflections

Physical Wellness

Judges 14:9
"When he returned later…he turned aside to look at the carcass of the lion, a swarm of bees and honey were in the body of the lion. He scraped the honey into his hand and went on, eating as he went."

Week Twenty-Two   **Day Five**

Not everything we do is good for us. There are things we can eat that do not agree with us. There are physical exertions that stress us too much. There are spiritual ideas that we need to stay away from. The world is full of things we need to be leery of.

It is our responsibility to know how to grow mentally, spiritually and physically in the correct direction. Trial and error is part of that process. God's laws is another way to ensure we are going in the right direction.

Here we find Sampson eating honey out of the body cavity of a dead lion. He had killed that lion earlier in his journeys and now bees were living there. Honey is good right? Yes, it's been considered the perfect food by some. So it ought to be good for our physical well-being, right?

Not so for Sampson. Moses in Numbers 6:6, instructs God's people that anything that touches a dead body is considered unclean. To make matters worse, the Nazirite vow that Sampson took forbade it as well.

So, there are limits to what we can do for our physical wellness. It seems like a small thing but we will not be blessed by God if we are not acting according to His instructions. He has reasons for what He asks of us. We do not have to understand them or even like them, we just need to be obedient regardless.

Reflections

Fellowship

Psalms 42:4
"I pour out my soul within me, for I used to go along with
the throng and lead them in procession to the house of God,
with the voice of joy and thanksgiving,
a multitude keeping festival."

Week Twenty-Two   **Day Six**

This verse comes from a very popular Psalm. It is written for the singers in the temple choir. The writer is exiled in the far north of Palestine and yearns to return to the temple in Jerusalem. The writer has a desire to go back to a place where he used to worship God with other believers.

He was apparently a leader within the fellowship. He longs to join the group again. He relates the joy and thanksgiving he felt as part of that group. Wherever he is at the time of the writing he is isolated and certainly remembers the need for fellowship.

I know how he feels. I miss my family, friends and church folks when I have prolonged times away. They are part of my life. They aide in my spiritual development. They are necessary in my life so I will be at peace and contented.

We all have a life to live. We cannot always be among friends and family. There are times when we must be away for whatever reason. It is helpful for me to have these longings for fellowship. It reminds me of how necessary it is.

I know it is not good for me to be alone too long in my own head. I have a tendency to isolate myself from others. The fellowship is important in my life to help me stay balanced. The fellowship feeds and nurtures me. I must make intentional efforts to be in the fellowship whenever possible.

Reflections

Service

Luke 14:33
"No one of you can be My disciple who does not give up all his own possessions."

Week Twenty-Two   **Day Seven**

Often you hear on the news that some rich, well-to-do, successful person has given up their lofty life and simplified it. They quit what they have been doing and take on a simple, less hectic lifestyle. The news media makes a big deal of this. They praise the concept and the actions of these people. The media touts these actions as revolutionary and unique.

You do not have to read too far into the teachings of Jesus to find these ideas have been around for a long time. Jesus knew the stuff of the world would entangle us. He knew we humans would take the way of the world. He preached this simple unobstructed lifestyle from the beginning, just look at the Beatitudes in Matthew's rendering of the Sermon on the Mount.

If we are to be of service to God, we must not allow the worldly idols to be our goals. We cannot follow the trappings of the world and God as well. Serving others as God instructs is not the same as serving ourselves. Self-care is important but only as a way to stay in the correct posture before God.

It's easier said than done, I know. I had to learn the lesson myself and am glad now I see it God's way. My life is simple and I intentionally work to keep it that way. Peace come from being obedient to God, only.

Reflections

Worship

Acts 20:7
"On the first day of the week...
we gather together to break bread."

Week Twenty-Three   **Day One**

Meeting together on the first day of the week to break bread was a very important time for these Christians. They began the week with worship, followed by the Lord's supper. What a marvelous way to start the week! We see here the importance of worship: this is the way early Christians started afresh each week. Today, we get together on Sundays as well. We are to begin our week getting together to worship our King!

I know all too well how easy it is to skip church. We look for that extra time for sleep or to get chores done. This is how we are setting the tone for our week, and also demonstrating what's really important to us! And when we do go to church, we let the Holy Spirit prepare our hearts, minds, and souls ready for whatever God has in store for us.

Reflections

Bible Reading

Revelation 22:19a
"If anyone takes away from the Words of the book of
prophecy..."

Week Twenty-Three   **Day Two**

Remember the game we all used to play in school that started with the teacher whispering in one kid's ear and then that kid in turn would whisper what was heard to the next kid and so on and so on until the last kid was told? The last kid would then repeat what was whispered and always the message received was nothing like the original whispered statement. That game never gets old and it serves as a wonderful example of how statements get distorted the more, they are passed along. The more folks that are told, the more the original meaning and intent is lost in the process. It is comical but a sad commentary of how we humans tend to add or subtract meaning to the messages we receive.

God understood that this principle would hold true even in the spreading of His Word throughout the ages. In the Book of Revelation 22:19, John writes a warning about this very human trait. He says that "If anyone takes away from the words of the book of prophecy, God shall take away..." This quote specifically refers to the revelation God gives to John in the Book of Revelation but the warning stands for all of God's Word. When we write, quote, speak or reference God's Word in any way, we need to do so accurately. God has guarded His Word throughout the generations and expects us to safeguard it as well.

Reflections

Prayer

Philemon 1:4
"...always offering prayer with joy in my
every prayer for you all..."

Week Twenty-Three   **Day Three**

Prayer is one of the ways we communicate with God. It is a time to acknowledge Him in our lives, a time to ask, a time of confession, a time of sharing. It is also a time to offer thanks - with joy. All too often I forget this. I come to Jesus whining and pleading and complaining. I am so grateful that He puts up with me! But I forget to tell Him even that!!

Everyday there are so many things that I experience that brings joy to my heart. Sharing these times with my Father should be one of those things. Let's be more mindful today in coming to the Lord with thanksgiving and joy.

Reflections

Meditation

Isaiah 1:18
"Come now, let us reason together, says the LORD:
though your sins are like scarlet, they shall be as white as
snow; though they are red like crimson,
they shall become like wool."

Week Twenty-Three   **Day Four**

This Scripture today is such a fantastic verse to meditate on. There is so much there. Scarlet and crimson are red colors from dyes held in great importance in ancient cultures. Dyes are not just colorful, but they must be colorfast, slow to fade or wash away. Our sins are like a good dye: colorful and slow to fade away. But God tells us that He is powerful and loving and amazing enough to completely remove the dye – the glaringly red stain – from our lives, leaving us completely free of those sins.

So, as you meditate today, think about what this verse means to you. What is God telling you? Really open your mind and heart up to that dialog. Really *hear*. And thank Him for sticking in there with you!

Reflections

Physical Wellness

Acts 27:34
"Therefore I urge you to take some food.
For it will give you strength, for not a hair is to perish from
the head of any of you."

Week Twenty-Three   **Day Five**

Charlie says that "we have to take whatever steps necessary to exercise our bodies sufficiently to keep them suitable for God's work" (*When Life Shows Up*, p. 205). He goes on to describe our bodies as vessels and points out that if a vessel is "broken, cracked, leaky, or otherwise not able to perform the function it is designed for" (p. 206), they are useless. That's a sobering thought. God has given me the gift of being very active and has used that activeness throughout my life and in my ministries. As I get older, I'm realizing that things just don't work like they used to. I am becoming painfully aware that I have to take extra care and caution to keep just the physical body in shape and at the level of activeness needed. That means doing "old lady stuff" like wearing socks with the things on the bottom to prevent slipping (and breaking a hip), taking vitamins, getting daily cardio, and understanding the importance of keeping some muscle tone. On the days I want to throw in the towel and "just be old" I think about the duty assignments God has for me to do. Then I get all excited with renewed energy!

Reflections

Fellowship

Revelation 22:9
"But he said to me, 'Do not do that. I am a fellow servant of yours and of your brethren the prophets and of those who heed to words of the book. Worship God.'"

Week Twenty-Three   **Day Six**

I found, in studying this Scripture, there is a very strong, yet subtle message. First of all, the verses surrounding this one describe life in New Jerusalem and then segues onto Jesus' return (and is the tail-end of John's vision of the future). For whatever reason (intentional or spontaneously), John fell down at this angel's feet and started to worship him. I can't say that I might not hit my knees if an angel appeared in real life!

Here's the subtle part: despite the holiness and awesomeness I would think angels exude, they aren't God. At all. And the angel gently reminds us who the only being is that we worship and bow down to. God. Worship God.

Reflections

Service

Job 36:11
"If they hear and serve Him, they will end their days in
prosperity and their years in pleasure."

Week Twenty-Three   **Day Seven**

I've said this before and I'll say it again: rewards are not the reason we do service work, but they're there! When we are in God's favor and are following His Words, good things tend to happen. Maybe not immediately and maybe not in the ways our little human brains conjure up, but I promise you, "prosperity and years in pleasure" do happen.

I don't think there has ever been a time when my heart was in the right place and I was outside of myself, thinking about others, that I have I left feeling empty or regretful. Every time I leave thinking to myself, "Man, I feel great! I know I'm getting more out of this than the recipient." Yes, service to others is almost always inconvenient and puts us outside of our comfort zones, but spending time doing God's work ultimately is the sweetest place to be.

Reflections

Worship

Joshua 24:15
"…choose for yourselves today whom you will serve: whether the gods which your fathers served which were beyond the River, or the gods of the Amorites in whose land you are living; but as for me and my house,
we will serve the Lord."

Week Twenty-Four   **Day One**

This scripture really needs none of my simple commentary. Joshua is wrapping up his time as leader of God's people. They have entered the Promised Land and wrenched away territory from the inhabitants of the land. There is still more work to do but Joshua is finished with his leadership role.

As the Book of Joshua closes, he gives those who will listen some final advice. He has led the stubborn people for a while now and even before that he was Moses' aide-de-camp, so he knows them well. He knows without a doubt as soon as the reins are loosed the people will go about doing something that will not please God.

Joshua asks them to make a choice: serve God or follow in the footsteps of the nations they just conquered. Look how well it turned out for those nations: our God destroyed them. Make a choice. Joshua says he and his family are on the side of God and will follow Him.

Easy, right? Not so much. History shows the people of God were disobedient almost instantly after the time of Joshua. We too are given this choice. Daily we can choose who we will worship. Look back on the days you chose God and see how they turned out. Compare them to the days you did not choose God. I'm just saying!

Reflections

Bible Reading

2 Timothy 2:7
"Consider what I say, for the Lord will give you
understanding in everything."

Week Twenty-Four   **Day Two**

There is nothing like walking into a situation and being totally surprised. Even if it is a surprise party for you, it is still disorienting when everyone jumps out and yells surprise! That, after all, is a pleasant dilemma to work through, but what of those surprises that are not so pleasant? For example, the extravagant phone bill, unplanned vehicle repair or my personal favorite, the emergency home water heater replacement, surprise! Still even a more distressful situation comes when the phone rings and the doctor relates some medical news, or the school principle reports misbehavior perpetrated by one of your kids.

The Apostle Paul understood this concept and made sure to let his protégé Timothy in on a secret. In 2 Timothy 2:7, Paul tells Timothy, "Consider what I say, for the Lord will give you understanding in everything." It is not for us to know all the ways of God but it is His desire to keep us in the loop when He feels we need it or can understand the big picture. One of His means of revelation is through the reading of His Word. God will use your daily Bible reading to enlighten you with His reasoning and to give you understanding.

Reflections

Prayer

Philippians 4:6
"Be anxious for nothing, but in everything by prayer and supplication with thanksgiving let your requests be made known to God."

Week Twenty-Four   **Day Three**

I know that not everyone had the loving Christian upbringing I had. I always had food, shelter and clothes. I went to church and to school. I had extracurricular opportunities as I grew up. I had two parents, a brother and a sister. I learned to swim, ride a bike, throw a baseball, football and play tennis. What a blessed upbringing.

I felt very little anxiety as a kid. When I was in trouble and a spanking was due, I got antsy but for the most part my life was protected and I was cared for. I really had no clue about the big bad world and the pitfalls that were possible. I guess a little naive for the most part.

God wants us to feel like I did growing up. Paul is writing to the Philippians this exact concept. Christianity is a new concept. The old law was burdensome and hard to follow. God wants us not to be anxious, to turn to Him and prayer. He wants us to allow Him to help us through whatever is going on in our lives. God is easy to reach; He is everywhere and He wants our interaction with Him. Anxious? Give God a call!

Reflections

Meditation

Job 23:7
"There the upright would reason with Him;
and I would be delivered forever from my judge."

There is nothing like getting blamed for something you did not do. Ask me, I know. Read my books that outline my unjust treatment by the legal system. Ultimately, I went to prison as an innocent man for a horrible crime. I spent five years in prison surrounded by folks who would seek to harm me and would have if God had not protected me.

Job, like myself, just wanted someone to hear what he was saying. He just wanted someone to see his actions from his point of view. It is so frustrating when the jury comes back and obviously did not hear a word you said. Or worse, did not believe a word you said.

In this part of the Book of Job, he wants to plead his case like He was in court. He wants to present evidence like a lawyer would to a judge and jury. He is frustrated that his friends seem to be oblivious to his claim of innocence. I feel his pain and frustration.

Meditation is important. That is when God helps you sort through these kinds of trials. You may still not like the outcome but you know for sure someone heard you. The God of the universe is more than happy to discuss anything you want. Right or wrong, He listens and will be there for you during the whole trial. He was there for me during the three-year court battle and during the five years of prison. Thank you, God.

Reflections

Physical Wellness

Esther 4:16
"Go assemble…fast for me; do not eat or drink for three days, night or day and I and my maidens also will fast in the same way."

Week Twenty-Four   **Day Five**

Have you ever watched anyone who was getting ready to perform for an audience? Athletes, singers, musicians, even debaters, one thing they all have in common is they warm up. Before the event they all practice, stretch, limber up, whatever it takes to get their minds, bodies and spirits ready for the event.

Esther is getting ready to go to the king and ask for a favor. The rules of the day were pretty black and white. If the king wanted you in his presence that was good. If he did not then he could have you killed. The Bible tells us the King was her husband and she was his favorite. Nevertheless, it was still a time of great danger for her.

Knowing that she was going to have to approach the King, she did what anyone else who has ever had to compete, perform or just stand in the gap, she got ready. She asked her uncle Mordecai to get his friends to fast and pray and she and her staff would do the same thing.

Physical wellness is a lifestyle choice. Fasting and praying are two ways to get your mind, body and spirit in the correct place for whatever situation you face. If you are consistently doing these things then you will be ready "When Life Shows Up."

Reflections

Fellowship

1 Thessalonians 3:2
"We sent Timothy, our brother and God's fellow worker in
the gospel of Christ, to strengthen and encourage you to
your faith…"

Week Twenty-Four   **Day Six**

I have always appreciated Paul's concern for the people of God. He was always mindful of their needs and the conflicts that would arise in their life due to this new Christian journey. The Mosaic laws were being used as a club to beat them down and God's way through the death of Jesus was so much different.

As a Pastor I often took on the burdens of my congregation. There was always a need, a prayer request, a death and a trial of some sort. Often, I felt overwhelmed. As a rural Pastor I felt like I was alone at times trying to serve all these needs. There was no staff, secretaries or associate pastors I could lean on.

Paul felt this way often as well. He did have Timothy to send to take some of these things off his mind. The fellowship he had with Timothy helped him lessen the burdens he was carrying. This letter was written while he was locked up. He had fellowship members helping him there as well.

This journey is not one we are supposed to do on our own. We are encouraged through God's Word to come alongside each other and shoulder each other's burdens. Paul benefited from these relationships and we will as well. Allow God to bring help around you. He knows your needs and what it will take to care for you. Fellowship is His way of blessing you.

Reflections

Service

Nehemiah 6:15
"So, the wall was completed…in fifty-two days."

Week Twenty-Four   **Day Seven**

I was getting ready for college. I was a senior in high school and filling out college applications. I had taken my SATs and the scores were sent to three colleges I was interested in. My scores were hopelessly mediocre but I managed to do well enough for the colleges to send me entrance applications. Who knew, right?

I was a high school kid, busy with school, sports and friends. This application process seemed arduous and complicated. I certainly did not want to take the time to fill out all the information they wanted. Not to mention why they even needed my first grade teacher's name and all that.

My Dad told me, after a griping session, something that stuck with me. Amazing right? He asked me, "How do you eat an elephant?" The answer was, "one bite at a time." Even the impossible could be accomplished just taking one step at a time.

Nehemiah was the governor of the remnant of God's people who were streaming back to Jerusalem from the Babylonian captivity. One of the goals was to rebuild the walls of the city. They were able to do that in fifty-two days. Remarkable and certainly a God thing.

The important lesson was they did it one block at a time and they did it together. No secret here, just people serving each other with God leading them.

Reflections

Worship

Joshua 24:22
"…You are witnesses against yourselves that you have chosen
for yourselves the Lord, to serve Him."

Week Twenty-Five   **Day One**

To me, this verse screams out that not only have we chosen the Lord on our own volition and vowed to serve Him, but we are to hold each other accountable for this decision. This, of course, only applies to those who have actually chosen to follow Jesus Christ. When we worship, we come together as like-minded souls and, in community, show our love and reverence toward Him with each other.

God is a relational being. As are we. We read in the Bible, verse after verse, about His desire for us to come together and worship our God together. This is repeated often because it is important. Oswald Chambers says our only purpose is to maintain a relationship with God. After that, He determines how we serve. Making a decision to serve Him is a choice to be held accountable by Him.

Reflections

Bible Reading

Philippians 2:16a
"Holding fast the Word of life…
cause to glory because I did not run in vain…"

Week Twenty-Five　　　　　　　　　　　　　　**Day Two**

In life there needs to be goals put in place to help direct our actions. Where there are no goals there is no seeable path and consequently loosely restricted actions that amount to very little productivity. If there is something to shoot for, that tends to direct actions toward the desired behavior. Yes, we need to live "one day at a time" but we still need to have a plan for the few things in life we can actually control. Rigidity needs to be avoided but seeking to be good stewards of our God given resources is a must.

In the Apostle Paul's letter to the church in Philippi, he stresses the needs for this type of foresight. He says in Philippians 2:16 that which he was, "Holding fast the Word of life, so that in the day of Christ I may have cause to glory because I did not run in vain nor toil in vain." No sense running around in circles because our actions are going to be judged. The Bible is specific about what God expects for us and there will be no excuses allowed at judgment time. We have a template for our actions already available, we just need to take responsibility and fit our actions into the pre-described expectations from God.

Reflections

Prayer

Colossians 1:12
"Giving thanks to the Father who has qualified us to share
in the inheritance of the saints in Light."

Week Twenty-Five   **Day Three**

Wow! What a powerful thing to be thankful for: "the inheritance of the saints in Light"!! Our God is an awesome God. He doesn't fool around when demonstrating His absolute love for us. I forget that sometimes. I forget how gracious and generous and completely perfect He is. I also forget to thank Him for it. In a world where we frantically search for love, we forget that it is right in front of us...or all over us.

Let's just pause right now and thank our Father.

Reflections

Meditation

Proverbs 25:8
"Do not go out hastily to argue your case…"

Week Twenty-Five   **Day Four**

It's a "me, me, me" world we live in. It's so easy to get caught up in who's wronged us, who owes us, and plainly saving face. All the time. This proverb warns us to avoid doing this. Instead, we should take time to listen – really listen – to what we're being told. And then, we meditate. Yep. Meditate. These are the situations we are to meditate upon. When we open our hearts and minds to the Holy Spirit, we are in a unique situation of potential clarity and love. As we think about the conflict, we are able to consider the other's point of view, how our point of view differs, how to deal with it, and also if we should even respond. When we meditate, the Holy Spirit will show us how to handle the situation in a manner that is pleasing to Him.

Reflections

Physical Wellness

1 King 17:13
"Do not fear…make me a little bread cake from it first…
afterward make one for yourself and for your son."

Week Twenty-Five   **Day Five**

Why don't I have this printed out in my work-out area? Mainly because I don't have a work-out area. You know what I mean, though, don't you? This is the kind of verse you'd find in Proverbs: total truth and terrific advice.

I love how it says "[discipline] yields peaceful fruit." It makes getting and staying in good physical wellness worth it, huh? I'm being facetious, of course, but the point is we are rewarded all the time for doing what is good and pleasing to our Father. He asks of us, rewards us hugely, and yet we still whine and moan. Therefore, Victoria and friends, lift you drooping hands, get off your butt, and strengthen your bones!

Reflections

Fellowship

1 Corinthians 12:14
"For the body is not one member, but many."

Week Twenty-Five   **Day Six**

Paul uses the human body to illustrate how the church should be. The church, like the body, is one organism with many critical and diverse parts. Paul starts the illustration with an explanation of the gifts the Holy Spirit gives each of us and how each of those gifts define our purpose within the church. Just as our body is made up of organs and tissues and cells that each have an essential role to play in the functioning of the body, so our church is made up of people that have essential roles to play in the functioning of the church. The body needs each member to do its part in order to work properly. When we fellowship together, we are to encourage each other to use the gifts our God gave to do the work He assigned us.

Reflections

Service

Ezra 1:2
"The Lord, the God of heaven…
has appointed me to build Him a house…"

Week Twenty-five   **Day Seven**

A little background: Although Assyria conquered Babylon in 721 B.C., it later fell to the Babylon Empire in 606 B.C. In 586 B.C., Nebuchadnezzar, of the Babylonian Empire, brought Jerusalem to its final demise, banishing its citizens. In 538 B.C., Cyrus of Persia conquered Babylon. That's about where Ezra picks up.

The importance of this passage is that Cyrus fulfills a prophecy of Jeremiah's (Jeremiah 25:1-12): Cyrus invites the exiled Jews back to rebuild Jerusalem and the temple. Before the beginning of time, God had planned for Cyrus to rebuild His house. Cyrus, obviously, could have ignored this service assignment, but he didn't. (Had he, God most definitely would have offered it to someone who would.) When we are faced with a service opportunity, we must remember that this is an assignment in which we were hand-picked by God to carry out. I'm telling you; service work is important!

Reflections

Worship

2 Samuel 7:23
"What one nation on earth is like Thy people Israel, whom God went to redeem for Himself as a people and to make a name for Himself…"

Week Twenty-Six   **Day One**

In the recovery circles we talk about the "pink cloud." It's that feeling of euphoria one gets as they come out of the fog of addiction, the feeling of ecstasy knowing that finally you are on the correct road and life is getting better. It's naïve in a way but a better outlook on life than whenever you can remember.

Some in that fellowship says that will not last. The reality of life will catch up with you. Being sober does not solve all your problems. Those are well-meaning people for the most part. The issue is life is still complicated: getting sober is just one step in getting better. Some of that is true but for me every day sober is better than any day before that time.

David is not talking about a "pink cloud." He says we worship a God that has no equal. We can stay full of joy, peace and contentment. Regardless of our circumstances our God will always be there to make our lives meaningful if we let Him. Great lesson, David.

Reflections

Bible Reading

Ephesians 6:11
"Put on the full armor of God, that you may be able to stand firm against the schemes of the devil."

Week Twenty-Six   **Day Two**

Everywhere you turn there is something bad happening. There are earthquakes, floods, forest fires, tornadoes and hurricanes. Corporate crime is always on the rise, health care professionals are stealing from us as well as the insurance companies, banks, pill companies and the United States government. Closer to home, violent crime is getting worse, gun usage and assaults are all over the news. Every person over the age of twenty-five has experienced some sort of traumatic event in their life, be it personal, a family member or a friend.

There is just no getting away from the madness caused by the sinful nature of the human race. The Apostle Paul had the same experience in his era and foresaw no change in the future. In his letter to the church at Ephesus he relates the only way to be sure, no matter what happens, that you will be ready. In Ephesians 6:11 he tells us to "Put on the full armor of God, that you may be able to stand firm against the schemes of the devil." Paul knew that God's Word was the only way to be certain that we could be ready for the challenges that would face us as Christians. It is not the local news media or the self-help gurus, God's Word alone is the answer.

Reflections

Prayer

Jude 1:20
"Beloved, building yourselves up on your most holy faith;
praying in the Holy Spirit…"

Week Twenty-Six   **Day Three**

There are just some things that never work. Like the stuff you buy from the TV. Never do they seem to work like advertised. For example, the toys you buy at Christmas that need "some assembly." How well does that work out? Or the person you call for customer service named "Mike" and you know he is from a distant country and barely understands English. When inquiring, Why can I not get my Direct TV to work, Mike will be of little help.

Today we are reading scripture written by Jesus' little brother, Jude. It is a short book but his topic is important. He is writing to defend the teaching of the apostles from false teachers. False doctrines had been creeping into this newly established Christianity and was becoming very divisive. Jude is telling his readers they must contend earnestly for the faith.

Prayer works only if you are praying in the Holy Spirit. The Holy Spirit will guide you to want the things God wants for you. The Holy Spirit is the answer to all our problems. He is God within us. He will lead, guide and direct us in the way God wants us to go. He will not fail and will never lead us astray. There is nothing more dependable than being in God's will allowing the Holy Spirit to lead. Sorry, Mike.

Reflections

Meditation

Psalms 1:1
"How blessed is the man…his delight is in the law of the
Lord, and in His law, he meditates day and night."

Week Twenty-Six   **Day Four**

It is always nice when the boss comes up to you and says, "good job." We do not necessarily work for those kinds of accolades but they are nice when they come. Everyone likes being recognized for their efforts. Sadly, they do not come often. Not that they are not deserved; folks just do not take the time to give encouragement or recognition that is earned.

In our scripture today David is letting us know how we can always get recognition from God. The Author, Creator and Sustainer of the universe tells us that a man is blessed if he meditates on His Word. Easy, right? Just read God's Word, listen to the Holy Spirit as He helps you interpret it and think about it. What does it mean? How does it apply to me? Where do I go with this information? And so on, right?

Of all the stuff of the world that we feel demands our attention, this is what God says will bless us. So why do we spend so much time mulling over the things that are not guaranteed to bless us? That is why this is a spiritual discipline. We need to begin to be intentional about this. The outcome is a given!

Reflections

Physical Wellness

Luke 17:12, 14
"He entered a certain village, ten leprous men who stood at a distance met Him...and it came about that as they were going, they were cleansed."

Week Twenty-Six   **Day Five**

It is important that we maintain our physical wellness so that we can be ready to serve God in any way He directs. Seems like a simple concept but once again not a lot of folks see it that way. In fact, folks use their lack of physical wellness as an excuse not to be able to serve God and others. What?

I'm not trying to beat anyone up or shame anyone but the point is, when able, we need to be disciplining ourselves to be the best we can in this area of our life. God has a plan for us and service opportunities He wants us to engage in. It's sad when we cannot rise to the occasion because of our health.

These ten leprous men sought God out for healing. The point of the story is that only one was grateful for his healing. The other issue is that they knew somehow God could help them. It does not say they were Christians or super believers; they were just sick and wanted help.

My point is that if your physical wellness is an issue, take it to God. There are things we cannot cure through exercise and diet. Pills, doctors and holistic remedies may not cure what ails us. God can and will if it's part of His plan. Do not accept these physical limitations without checking with God. He knows what you need and if it is in His will, He will remove those limitations.

Reflections

Fellowship

2 Corinthians 6:14
"Do not be bound together with unbelievers; for what partnership have righteousness and lawlessness, or what fellowship has light with darkness?"

Week Twenty-Six   **Day Six**

If my parents told me once they told me a thousand times, "you are known by who you hang around with." So true! Of course, I did not want to believe them at the time. As I have grown, I know that I need to be careful about the company I keep.

It is not my right to judge. I do need to show some discernment and ascertain who will be helpful in my Christian journey and who will not. Jesus helped everyone, believers or not. He did not, however, have spend-the-night parties with them, or stay out all night in shady situations with them. He did not allow them to drag Him into compromising situations.

Paul is warning the folks in Corinth to be mindful of their associations. Bad will drag good down before good can pull bad up. Our reputations are important and we lose effective Christian witness if it gets tainted. Allow the Holy Spirit to teach you who, how long and what is necessary for each person you serve. We want to save the world, right? We must do so with discernment and God's guidance, not blindly as "do gooders."

Reflections

Service

Deuteronomy 26:14
"I have listened to the voice of the Lord my God; I have done according to all that Thou hast commanded me."

Week Twenty-Six   **Day Seven**

Moses is closing out his service to God's people. He is teaching this new generation the ways of God. Their parents are all dead, not allowed to enter the Promised Land. This new generation of believers will soon face the challenges of taking over the new land God has prepared for them. Moses knows their weaknesses and the tendencies to stray from God.

Here Moses is saying that the people have to examine themselves to ensure they have been doing what God asks them to do. Here specifically, it is tithing to the poor. They have been of service as they have been instructed. God must approve of what we do and who we are to serve. Our own ideas, though they may seem correct, must be right before God. He will let us know. We fall victim for wanting "good" when God wants the "best."

It is not in God's will for us to do what we want. Not all needs out there in the world are for our attention. We are given gifts and resources for God's use, not our own. We will not be blessed if we are serving outside God's will.

Reflections

Worship

1 Kings 3:5
"God said, 'Ask for what you wish me to give to you.'"

Week Twenty-Seven   **Day One**

Charlie makes the bold statement on page 90 of his book, *When Life Shows Up*, that if you lack the *need* to gather with brothers and sisters of the Church, "you are dangerously unprepared for when life shows up." Pretty harsh proclamation. But if ever there were someone who knew the importance of this spiritual discipline, that would be brother Charlie. Had it not been for the army of believers he had surrounding him during the years of being dragged, humiliated, and scared through his legal goat-rope, I firmly believe Charlie would not have made it.

Building a solid, faithful support system of fellow Christians is absolutely imperative for any of us engaging in life. When the proverbial stuff hits the fan, we need to have our "peeps" in place – knowing full well that, not only will they stand beside us during tough times, they will carry us when we can't walk on our own. You usually don't get that kind of commitment overnight. So, make being with other Christians frequently – sharing the tough stuff as well as the praises – a top priority. It may quite literally save your life one day.

Reflections

Bible Reading

Week Twenty-Seven   **Day Two**

There seems to always be someone around who wants us to "do as they do." You know those folks who tend to want to drag us into their drama, their emergency or their particular world view. Some folks are not satisfied unless they have control over everyone around them. These folks are not bad people, they just want to have company in their way of thinking. The problem is that they will not stop at a polite "no thanks," that tends to make them want to start degrading your belief system, your way of life or your character.

Sadly, this happens in the church as well. Cliques form, factions develop and, for the sake of control, begin to pervert the truth of God's Word to the point where it is no longer an inerrant spiritual standard. The Apostle Paul tells us in Galatians 2:5, he "did not yield in subjection to them, for even an hour, so that the truth of the gospel, might remain…" God's Word is not to be compromised and the only way to combat those who seek to do so is to know it well enough to call them on their inaccuracies. God wants you to protect His Word and to pass it from generation to generation unsullied by human attempts to neutralize its power and authority.

Reflections

Prayer

Matthew 21:22
"And all things you ask in prayer, believing,
you will receive."

Week Twenty-Seven   **Day Three**

It's so easy to fall into the false notion that if we have enough faith, anything we pray for will be granted. As if! Prayer doesn't work that way. God isn't a mythical genie. However, He is a powerful God. 1 John 5:14 tells us, "...if we ask anything *according to His will*, He hears us." Did you catch that? According to His will. That's the key: to pray for God's will to be done.

So, when we pray that a co-worker comes to some horrible demise, we can be pretty confident that this isn't what God wants. However, when we change that prayer – and really mean it – to ask God to help us show love and patience to that co-worker, we can be pretty confident that this is what God wants. When we start to adopt the mind of Christ, we align more perfectly with God.

Reflections

Meditation

Nehemiah 9:20
"You gave Your good Spirit to instruct them, Your manna
You did not withhold from their mouth and You gave them
water for their thirst."

Week Twenty-Seven   **Day Four**

One of the fantastical things about the Bible, for me, is the strength and the plethora of stories that reassure me when I start to doubt God. The whole Israelites wandering the desert for 40 years is one of those tales. God sequestered these people because they disobeyed Him and worshipped other gods. God put the Israelites in timeout, for a long time, under dicey conditions. But He was with them – every one of them – the whole time. He showed them were to go; He provided food every single morning; He took care of their needs. And the Jewish nation learned about the might and sovereignty of God; they learned to trust Him and depend on Him, follow Him and worship only Him.

Well, God certainly hasn't ever dropped manna on my lawn when He's put me in timeout! But what He has dropped on my lawn is unexpected funds to use to pay bills that had piled up; He has provided me unbelievable comfort and peace even during my darkest hours; He has been faithful and, well, there! I'm not sure I would be as cognizant of this had I not known about the exiled Jews and what He did for them. He is our everything. Always.

Reflections

Physical Wellness

1 Corinthians 9:35
"Every athlete exercises self-control in all things. They do it to receive a perishable wreath, but we are an imperishable."

Week Twenty-Seven   **Day Five**

Here Paul focuses on the attributes needed for an athlete to succeed in the popular Olympic games. He goes on to explain that anyone who competes in these games must employ self-control in all areas of their lives. These athletes must maintain a strict diet and adhere to a punishing training schedule designed to push both their mental and physical limits. And all this for a "perishable wreath."

So the question begs: what strict diet and training schedule do we adhere to in order to receive everlasting life with God? What areas of our lives do we show self-control? How do we prepare ourselves, physically and mentally, for the long haul? Every believer of the Lord Jesus Christ who employs such discipline and self-control – for the sake of Christ Jesus – is automatically promised an everlasting and indestructible wreath. What a reward!

Reflections

Fellowship

Zephaniah 2:1
"Gather yourselves together, yes gather...without shame..."

Week Twenty-Seven   **Day Six**

I've certainly been through times in my life in which I wanted to isolate and hide from the world because of some bad decision I made. Church was the absolute last place I wanted to go. I imagined the condescending looks and whispers and holier-than-thou attitudes. And, yes, sometimes that does happen. But God intended the body of Christ to be the place we run to when we're in such a state. It is to be a place of grace and love and understanding.

Not only are we to use fellowship to help get us through tough times, we are also charged with providing that church God intended - one where others run to when they're in a pickle. That means we are to exude grace and love and understanding - everything we would want when the roles are reversed.

Reflections

Service

John 4:7
"There came a woman of Samaria to draw water.
Jesus said to her, 'Give Me a drink.'"

Week Twenty-Seven   **Day Seven**

This is an example of another time someone was asked to do something for God and was obedient. This particular story is powerful in that the interaction between the Samaritans and the Jews was adversarial. Additionally, Samaritans were considered "unclean" and this particular woman was not held in high regards by her own people. But yet, there's our Christ, encouraging her with His love and grace.

As a result, He breaks through her tough exterior and she comes to accept Christ as her Savior, bringing a whole host of neighbors with her. When we are asked to do something for God, He always has an ulterior motive. He uses each of us to help show His love, grace, and forgiveness to others which, in turn, brings them to know Him.

Reflections

Worship

Romans 1:25
"They exchanged the truth of God for a lie and worshipped
and served the creature rather than the Creator,
who is blessed forever. Amen."

Week Twenty-Eight   **Day One**

There are lots of things in this world that attract my attention. I look at lakes and wonder how deep they are. I look at shopping malls and wonder how many people pass through there in a day, week, month or year. I wonder how Tiger Woods can hit a golf ball so far. Or what ever happened to Jimmy Connors, the tennis player?

I have a new interest today, the stars. I have this Star Application on my phone. I turn it on, point my phone to the sky and the application will show me what I am looking at - what star, planet or constellation. I am so impressed with the technology.

What Paul is telling me in the verse is that I need not be impressed with the technology. I need to be impressed with the God who made the stars, the planets and formed the constellations. I know Paul is correct. God made everything!

I am humbled by the vastness of God's creation. I worship Him because not only did He make the universe and all that is in it, He loves me. He made me to love Him back.

Reflections

Bible Reading

Proverbs 30: 6
"Do not add to His Words, lest He reprove you,
and you be proved a liar."

Week Twenty-Eight   **Day Two**

When I was in the seventh grade, I had a friend who thought he knew everything, a good guy and a great friend but sometimes hard to take. Not only did he know everything but he was always trying to "one up" someone else. Everything he had was better than everyone else's. Everything he did was better than what you did. The facts never did bear out these claims but, in his mind, that's the way the world was. So most of the guys in our group of friends just ignored this quirk and made the best of it. As kids our responsibility or circle of influence was not so influential that this type of attitude became an agent for mass change.

Plenty of adults do the same thing as well. Their need to be superior transcends into all areas of life. Some adults become influential enough that when they play the "one up" game, minds get changed. In some cases that is no big deal because things of little importance are affected. However, care needs to be given when matters of God's Word are bantered about. In Proverbs 30:5, 6, the wise man says, "Every word of God is tested…do not add to His words, lest He reprove you…" We put ourselves in a bad position before God if we do not handle His Word with the proper respect, reverence and accuracy.

Reflections

Prayer

Mark 2:10
"In order that you may know that the Son of Man has the authority on earth to forgive sins."

Week Twenty-Eight   **Day Three**

My Dad was a smart guy. I used to hate when he corrected my homework. I would get the benefit of his vast knowledge on whatever subject he was correcting. I just wanted to go out and play, right or wrong was all I was ever looking for. I really did not want to waste a lot of time on a lecture, actually learning something.

Jesus was the master of "teachable moments." He took every opportunity to teach those who would listen. He wanted us to know about Him, His mission on earth and His Father in heaven. He took the time to explain His actions so those around Him could learn.

In this case He has healed a man with paralysis. He could have just looked at the man and he would have been healed. He wanted those gathered around to know that He, the Son of God, had the power to forgive sins on earth. He could have said, get up and walk but that would not have conveyed the message He wanted.

We pray because we want to learn from God. He could just fix things, heal folks, make problems go away. He does not because He wants us to learn some lessons. He allows us to go through things to draw us close to Him. Prayer helps us sort out these lessons.

Reflections

Meditation

Ezra 6:21
"The sons of Israel…who separated themselves from the
impurity of the nations of the land to join them,
to seek the Lord God of Israel, ate the Passover."

Week Twenty-Eight   **Day Four**

To listen for God's Word in our life we must be in the correct posture before Him. If the din of the world is constantly bombarding our senses, we will have a hard time hearing God's still, small voice. God is not going to shout over the world's noise. He is not going to compete with the chatter of man's self-ego.

Ezra led one of the groups from their place of exile back to Jerusalem. That group joined a group that was already there. The group that they joined had purposely kept themselves away from the residents of the land who were engaged in heathen practices. Ezra was dedicating the temple and preparing for the Feast of the Passover.

It is important for us to learn that we must separate ourselves at times from the noise of the world. Obviously, we live in the world and have to take part in the normal commerce in order to survive. For us to grow spiritually we must make time to separate ourselves to commune with God, to have conversations and to listen for instructions.

We must learn to discern those things of the world that help us draw closer to God and those that do not. Ezra knew this dedication and feast were important for their spiritual growth and ensured he led his people to a position before God so that these times would be pleasing to Him.

Reflections

Physical Wellness

1 John 4:4
"Greater is He that is in you than he that is in the world"

Week Twenty-Eight   **Day Five**

From the time we get up in the morning until we go to bed at night there is a battle going on. The ruler of the world is Satan and he wants us to stumble, fall and curse God. The Holy Spirit, who is in us, wants us to grow spiritually and draw close to God.

If we are doing destructive things mentally, spiritually or physically we give Satan an opportunity to defeat us. Every time a Christian stumbles it is not only destructive to the individual, it is destructive to Christianity as a whole. The world wants to point to fallen believers and say the whole group is bad.

John is warning his readers that there are false, lying teachers out there trying to make us stumble. He is encouraging the believers. He wants them to know that the Holy Spirit in us is greater than the Evil One directing these false, lying teachers.

We must take care to keep ourselves ready for these attacks. We must watch how we present ourselves so we are not seen as easy prey for the Evil One. Mostly we must remember that our bodies play host to the Holy Spirit. What kind of accommodations are you providing for the Holy Spirit?

Reflections

Fellowship

Nahum 1:7
"The Lord is good, a stronghold in times of trouble and He
knows those who take refuge in Him."

Week Twenty-Eight   **Day Six**

As a member of the Armed Forces we were taught that there are
no individuals. The team is what is important. Everyone on the
team has a job and without that job being done correctly the
team is not as strong. Many coaches have said, "There is no I
in team." The message is there: we must perform as a group,
no one person has enough ability to carry the group.

This scripture is so uplifting for me. There are times when
I am in need of shelter, protection and comfort. It is good to
know there are others who need it also. I am not alone with
my problems. Others have the same ones. I can take refuge
with the fellowship. I can cling to others who have walked the
path before me.

The best part is knowing God knows. He knows that we
believers are huddled with each other and why we are there.
He cares and purposely provided the fellowship to be a place
of comfort and refuge. There are no individuals in fellowship.
God provides for us all in the ways we need and we all need
God, alike.

Reflections

Service

Acts 2:42
"They were continually devoting themselves to the apostles' teaching and to fellowship to the breaking of bread and prayer."

Week Twenty-Eight   **Day Seven**

When Jesus ascended into heaven, He told His disciples that a great thing was about to happen. The Holy Spirit then indwelled them all. The Holy Spirit then began to lead them where Jesus left off.

The result was a community of believers who were willing to learn from the Apostles and share the burdens of life with each other. Luke does a great job letting us know how different this was than the culture that was already in place.

The Mosaic law was being used by the religious elite to bolster their individual status. It was not being used to point folks to God as originally intended. The new concept of fellowship and service was a refreshing change to these struggling believers.

It is the same way today. The world believes that individualism is a right and the only way to success. The Holy Spirit teaches us that to serve each other is the only way to be obedient to God. The life of service looks so different than what the world offers as a solution. The life of service is the only way to be in the correct posture before God. He wants us to be successful in our efforts to draw near to Him and service is the key.

Reflections

Worship

Isaiah 12:5
"Sing praises to the LORD, for He has done gloriously; let this be made known in all the earth."

Week Twenty-Nine   **Day One**

We hear more prayer requests and complaining about our lives in our Bible Studies and Small Groups, don't we? I'm certainly guilty. Why is it that I feel like I'm bragging when God has done something "glorious" in my life? Why is it that we tend to focus on the negative, almost completely excluding the positive?

Right here, the Bible tells us differently. We are to "sing praises" and let everyone know about the goodness. We owe it, not only to ourselves, but to those around us and, especially God! We have no problem bragging about advances our children/significant other, even ourselves, make. We go on and on and on.... And yet we don't afford that same exaltation for the supernatural things God does for us. What's up with that? As a community we need to boldly share God's greatness — even if it seems like bragging. Brag away! Our God deserves it!!

Reflections

Bible Reading

Psalms 143:10
"Teach me to do Thy will, for Thou art my God. Let Your good Spirit lead me on level ground."

Week Twenty-Nine   **Day Two**

One thing my parents were, was fair. They may have made me mad when I was growing up but they were always fair. It was always clear in my mind what the rules of the kingdom were. I never got in trouble for doing something that I did not know was right or wrong. The rules, boundaries and expectations were always made clear to me so that there would be no excuse if I exceeded them. I understood full well the cost of each infraction as laid out by my parents. At the time I thought they were strict but now I know they were just helping to value the realities of life.

In David's Psalm 143 he is asking God for that same kind of guidance. He wants to know the rules so that he will be sure to obey them and subsequently place himself in the correct posture before Him. In Psalms 143:10, he says to God, "Teach me to do Thy will, for Thou art my God, let Thy good Spirit lead me on level ground." David wanted to know the rules so he could do what was expected of him; we too need to do the same thing. God has provided an instruction manual to help us to just that. The Bible was given for the express purpose of helping us get to know God and His expectations for us.

Reflections

Prayer

Mark 14:38
"Keep watching and praying that you may not come into temptation, the spirit is willing, but the flesh is weak."

Week Twenty-Nine   **Day Three**

Jesus had just wakened Peter, James, and John who fell asleep after He asked them to stay awake. One job. Watch and pray. They couldn't even do that. How many times have you been in the same boat? You know what you're doing is not right, you know what you *should* be doing, and yet you still "fall asleep".

One of my favorite characters in the Bible is Paul. He's irritatingly confident in his faith and relationship with God. I just love it! One of the things he said (that is applicable to my life way too often) is, "I do not understand what I do. For what I want to do I do not do, but what I hate I do" (Romans 7:15). Later on in that chapter he reiterates this sentiment and adds, "...this I keep on doing" (Romans 7:19). I can so relate. I know that if Jesus came down and asked me to "watch and pray", I'd fall asleep too! There is no doubt in my mind. But that's what He's asked us to do: watch and pray. When we're watching and praying, Satan has less of a chance to tempt us as our eyes and hearts on are the King.

Reflections

Meditation

2 Chronicles 29:11
"My sons, do not be negligent now, for the Lord has chosen you to stand before Him, to minister to Him, and to be His ministers and burn incense."

Week Twenty-Nine   **Day Four**

Hezekiah was twenty-five when he became king of Judah. And things were a mess. He inherited a kingdom of people who had turned their faces and backs against God, basically shutting down the church and living a life of sin and debauchery. So, Hezekiah's first goal was to reestablish the church, realign with God, and do "what was right in the eyes of the Lord." I find that pretty impressive. And it speaks volumes for Hezekiah's reliance on a relationship with God. I'm sure it was not received well, either.

Hezekiah didn't care. The fact that his eyes were firmly focused on God and what God wanted, regardless of how "disruptive" and unpopular this decision was amongst his people, Hezekiah only had eyes for God. I wonder if I would handle it the same way. I wonder if my eyes are firmly on God and not on the popular current thinking. In my meditation time today, I certainly will listen to what God has to say on this.

Reflections

Physical Wellness

2 Peter 3:10
"But the day of the Lord will come as a thief in the night..."

Week Twenty-Nine   **Day Five**

False teachers are chiding Christians about the "supposed" return of Jesus. Apparently, they felt it needed to be then, in their lifetime, immediately. We know that didn't happen. Peter points out in the previous verse that God isn't slow or late, but instead is trying to give as much as possible the time and opportunity to turn to Him through their faith in Jesus Christ.

In this verse, Peter maintains that Jesus will indeed come, but warned that no one knows when this time is. No one. This is the reason we follow spiritual disciplines in our lives–to be prepared. This is the reason we worship and pray and meditate and serve and "get in shape" for His return. We truly don't want to be caught with our pants down.

Reflections

Fellowship

Micah 5:4
"And He will arise and shepherd His flock…"

Week Twenty-Nine   **Day Six**

Micah "gives a chilling lament of approaching judgment": his message is tinged with hope as he announces God's promise of restoration. That's how important we are to Him. The shepherd/flock analogy is all through the Bible, but it illustrates so clearly His love for us. Yes, He cares for each of us individually (He knows every hair on our heads!), but we are important as a whole.

Which is why fellowship is a spiritual discipline. It's that crucial. We must live our lives in community with one another and we must do it His way: with love, forgiveness, grace. Fellowship with others pleases God. Don't you love it when your children are all getting along and playing cooperatively with each other? That's what God wants.

Reflections

Service

Romans 1:1
"Paul, a bond-servant of Christ Jesus, called as an apostle,
set apart for the gospel of God."

Week Twenty-Nine   **Day Seven**

Letters, in Paul's times, followed a specific pattern: the writer identified himself, with the recipient listed next, followed by a formal greeting. In Paul's letter to the Romans, Paul identifies himself as the mission Christ has assigned to him. Being a bond-servant and follower of Christ was so important to Paul that it became part of his identifying characteristics. It is the way he described himself.

Can we describe ourselves based on the mission Christ assigns us? Are we known for our service work? God gives each of us a purpose and a task to be carried out for His glory. Like the different entities of a body, each of us have a job to do with the gifts we have been given to carry out that job. Through prayer, Scripture, meditation and talking with others, we find our mission. It is at that point whether we accept it or not.

Reflections

Worship

Hebrews 11:3
"By faith we understand that the worlds were prepared by
the word of God, so that what is seen was not made out of
things which are visible."

People struggle with the concept of faith. Most folks want to
see and touch something before they accept its value. Pretty
understandable, especially in the computer age where sounds
and sights can be manipulated so easily. We can reproduce
events digitally that look like something that really happened.
Of course, we also hear a lot of words coming from the mouths
of preachers, teachers, and government leaders that are empty,
not true or just self-serving.

The writer of Hebrews wants us to understand the power
that comes from faith in God. Chapter Eleven is the faith
chapter. I wrote a book based on the acts of faith these folks
in this chapter demonstrated for us, "I Don't Want to God!"
is the title.

Back in the Book of Joshua, Chapter 24, Verse 15, he
tells us to choose. Joshua chooses God to serve. This passage
is asking the same thing. We step out in faith often: in our
cars, on airplanes, in restaurants and in elevators, I could go
on. Here we are being told that God made everything out of
nothing and we can believe it or not. If we believe then He is
certainly worthy of our worship.

Reflections

Bible Reading

Psalms 78:1
"Listen, oh my people to my instructions; incline your ears
to the words of my mouth…"

Week Thirty   **Day Two**

I have a good friend that used to tell his young son, "I know my mouth is moving and words are coming out, why are you not moving?" It's a classic struggle for all of us who are parents. You know that you have just given instruction but there is some sort of disconnect or translation problem by the time it gets to your child's ears. We all tend to hear what we want to at times; likewise, we all let words go in one ear and out the other. It is hard at times to get into the habit of really listening to what is being said, especially when we develop the habit of just pretending to do so.

As adults we know that there is a difference in listening and hearing. Hearing implies a process of listening, analyzing the words and then forming an appropriate response or action. Hearing means that an understanding was reached and an action is to follow. Obviously not everything we listen to falls into the category of needing action. God's Words are always ones to be heard. In God's attempt to bring His unfaithful people back in line He tells them in Psalms 78:1, "Listen, O my people, to my instructions; incline your ears to the words of my mouth." He's pretty clear that God's Words are not like the others floating around in our world or even our heads.

Reflections

Prayer

Luke 1:19
"I am the angel Gabriel…I have been sent to you and to
bring you good news."

Week Thirty   **Day Three**

One of my favorite parts of the Bible is this scene in the temple. The angel Gabriel appears to the priest, Zechariah. He tells him he and his wife Elizabeth will be having a child soon. They were old and past the normal child conceiving and bearing years. They had prayed for a child and up to then their prayers seemed to have been unanswered.

Dr. Luke is relating a version of the birth narrative of Jesus. John the Baptist is eventually born to Zechariah and Elizabeth. Jesus said that there is no other person born of woman as great as John the Baptist. I guess he was worth the wait.

As a discipline, prayer can be frustrating. We do it and do it and at times nothing seems to happen. That is a defeated way to look at it. If you are praying, something is happening. You are communicating with God, that is a good thing. You are disciplining yourself to take time to put away worldly, daily pursuits and communicate with our Creator. The most important thing that is happening is that you are learning to wait on God.

Prayers are not wish lists we want God to fill. Prayer is communication that is designed to bring us closer to God. This older couple prayed, waited and God, when it was unexpected to them, answered their prayer. God knew all along the timing that was needed to answer their prayer in such a powerful way.

Reflections

Meditation

2 Kings 6:17
"O Lord, I pray, open his eyes that he may see."

Week Thirty   **Day Four**

My parents were not lazy. They actively participated in my life. I was always amazed about how much they knew. I was even more amazed at how accurately they could ascertain my actions. It seemed like I could do nothing they did not know about. Right or wrong, they seemed to have a sixth sense about my activities.

When I became a parent, I was actively involved in my son's life. He often thought the same thing about me. How do you know, Dad, what I was thinking? Why am I in trouble, he would think, he cannot possibly know what I did! He thought I had the same sixth sense.

The truth is, as you readers know, all kids in all generations are alike. What we did and thought is really not much different than what our parents thought and did. Experience is the key. Do things enough times and it just gets more clear and easier.

Elisha is praying that his servant will see that their current situation is not so dire. Elisha sees the heavenly army that is protecting them, the servant does not. Our meditation practices can help us see beyond our current situations. The more we do it the clearer we see our current situations. Keep practicing, it gets better.

Reflections

Physical Wellness

James 1:22
"Prove yourself doers of the word and not merely hearers
who delude themselves."

Week Thirty   **Day Five**

I've been around folks who say, "I'm the kind of person who...."
Folks are always wanting us to believe something they say. Yet,
there is no physical evidence of truth in their statement. We
are inundated by advertisements that want us to believe that
certain products can do certain things. People get on their
pedestals and pontificate their worth to society, urging others
to give money, please.

If you have to say you are a certain way then you probably
are not. If the evidence is not apparent in your actions then
most likely the claims are false. It's just a rule of thumb I use
to determine the validity of statements like that.

James gets this as well. Talking about yourself or what you
are going to do is of little to no use. The actions, the doing of
these statements are the proof. We can talk all day about how
we are going to get better at self-care but it is evident if we
are actually doing it. You do not think yourself into changes,
you act yourself into them. Keep up the good work, physical
wellness is a must to be able to walk as God would have us.
Actions, not words!

Reflections

Fellowship

Isaiah 65:25
"The wolf and the lamb shall graze together and the lion
shall eat straw like the ox…"

Week Thirty   **Day Six**

If you watch any science fiction shows there seems to be a lot of far-fetched ideas. I remember when the original Lost in Space TV series was running. I was a kid and the idea of a talking, lifesaving robot was neat, unbelievable but neat. All their adventures were fun to watch but even as a kid I knew it was just make-believe.

In today's passage, Isaiah is describing the characteristics of the future heavenly kingdom. One of the characteristics is that the animosity in nature will be removed. Creatures that have been incompatible will be fine with each other. God's creatures will be able to fellowship with each other.

Like a science fiction episode, it seems unbelievable. How can this be? In God's economy He has always wanted His creation to get along. We have all been created for a purpose and that is to help each other to take the earthly journey. No one has all the abilities to survive on their own. We need each other's gifts to survive.

If the lions can eventually lay down with the lambs in the future, we should be able to fellowship today. Isaiah is talking about the perfect new heaven and new earth. Things will be different but the present does not have to be so different. Is it so far-fetched to believe we can all get along as God planned? I do not think so. I have got to get out of my own way and let the Holy Spirit teach me to fellowship with those God intends me to.

Reflections

Service

1 Corinthians 1:10
"I exhort you, brethren, by the name of our Lord Jesus Christ, that you all agree and there be no divisions among you, but you be made complete in the same mind and in the same judgment."

Week Thirty   **Day Seven**

It's pretty hard for a sports team to win if they are at odds with each other. If they are not wanting the same thing there will be no victories on the playing field, court or track. Unless the team is united the divisions will keep their performance unsatisfactory to reach their goals.

As a servant of God, I must get on the same page with those who are called into service with me. If I want my way and no one else has a say, then I am doomed to be alone. Once alone I become ineffective in my service.

Paul is telling those folks in the church at Corinth the same thing. This spiritual battle cannot be won without the help of each other. We must stay committed to the same goals or we will not be successful. We must serve each other for a common end goal.

Paul uses the word "exhort" here. It's as strong a plea he can use. He understands their difficulties in living the life God has set for them. He also uses the word "complete." We have to be willing to serve the fellowship. It is not complete if we just think of ourselves.

Reflections

Worship

Week Thirty-One   **Day One**

One thing we can say with absolute certainty about our God is that He is loyal. To a fault, almost. While this Scripture is specifically talking about God's wrath with Babylon and its idols, we see here that God doesn't play around. Just as He is quick to reward us, He is as quick to judge and punish us.

Sometimes when things are going awry in my life and I am clueless to the cause of it, I simply need to remember the sin in my life. God doesn't tolerate it. He doesn't "get even" or lash out. His is a method of lovingly realigning His people with His will, and we must grasp the idea He is quick to act and will "fully repay" to bring us back into His fold. We are that important to Him.

Reflections

Bible Reading

Job 38:1
"The Lord answered Job out of the whirlwind."

Week Thirty-One   **Day Two**

As humans we all want to be heard! We want to be able to speak and have those around understand us. We want our words to be mulled over and despite what was actually said, have the meaning to be intuitively comprehended. Not psychic stuff but just basic acknowledgment of our feelings, hurts, joys, sadness and loneliness for example. We just have an inner need for others to have empathy for us as we travel through this life. Sadly, we are all so self oriented we rarely take time to show our true understanding or concern for what others go through. We just get so preoccupied with our own issues that we have no real energy to participate in the "stuff" of others.

Fortunately God is better than that. When we talk to Him, He is listening and understands our situation. In Job 38:1, the author tells us that, "The Lord answered Job out of the whirlwind…" Job had been going through some real tough stuff and had been holding onto his faith by his fingernails. He longed for confirmation from God that He was there and listening. God answered Job, did not actually tell him what he wanted to hear, but He did acknowledge his presence. God knows and cares for us as individuals. He does not lump us into a mass of humanity, we are all special and unique to Him.

Reflections

Prayer

Acts 6:4
"But we will devote ourselves to prayer
and to the ministry of the Word."

Week Thirty-One   **Day Three**

Years ago, I participated in a church-wide prayer time: prayer warriors signed up for the same hour every day to pray; so at least twenty-four people were praying every day. My timeslot was something like 3 o'clock in the morning. The person praying before me would call around 2:55 am, check in, and we'd pray together. Then I'd spend the next 50 minutes praying, calling the 4 o'clock person five minutes before to "pass the baton". It was one of the coolest things I've ever done. I can't remember how it ended, but I do know that I abandoned that timeslot in a heartbeat! Unfortunately, I have not kept up a regular prayer time since.

I know that the goal of the apostles was to devote their lives to prayer and spreading the Word, undistracted by everyday life. Most of us don't have the luxury to do that. However, each of us could certainly up our game. Let's make prayer more important in our daily lives; devote time to God.

Reflections

Meditation

2 Samuel 14:14b
"God does not take away life but plans ways so that the
banished one will not be cast out from Him."

Week Thirty-One   **Day Four**

The background story this verse comes from is a convoluted and intricate tale and is worth taking a moment, right now, to read (start with chapter 13). But for our purposes I will recap: Ammon, King David's son (yeah, *that* King David) coveted his sister, Tamar, and ends up raping her. Another of David's sons, Absalom, catches wind of what happened to Tamar, has Ammon killed and flees. David, the king, should be trying to get him returned and punished, but he doesn't because this wise woman from Tekoa pointed out that if God seeks out the banished to bring back into fold, why shouldn't David?

I say all that to say this: no one is insignificant to God. Absolutely, positively no one. That includes you. And me. It is so important to God for us to be with Him–always. He goes to extraordinary lengths to keep us near Him. Think about how utterly important and vital you are to God.

Reflections

Physical Wellness

Proverbs 31:17
"She dresses herself with strength
and makes her arms strong."

Week Thirty-One   **Day Five**

Proverbs 31 is chock-full of some really good how-to-be-a-good-person-of-God instruction with the first half focused on men and the second on women. It originally came from Lemuel's mom for the purpose of 1) giving him advice on how a king should reign, and 2) outlining the qualities of a good wife.

Interestingly, Lemuel's mama lists care of physical health as a characteristic of the ideal woman. Do you think God could be more subtle?! That's what we are being told here: physical wellness is essential. Again, this may look different from individual to individual but the outlining message is that we are to refrain from those things that harm us. Why? Because our physical health impacts our spiritual health and when our physical health is compromised or causes us to sin, our relationship with God gets messy. No one wants that.

Reflections

Fellowship

2 Timothy 3:12
"All who desire to live godly in Christ Jesus will be
persecuted."

Week Thirty-One   **Day Six**

One of the perks of fellowship is that we spend time with others who desire the same and have similar experiences to our own. Paul wrote this letter while he was in prison, awaiting an impending death for his faith. It must have been an incredibly stressful and worrisome time for him. By his own accord, Paul spent most of his time in prayer and meditation to help him through this period, but Paul also had the need for human interaction. He turned to those he fellowshipped with.

By spending time in fellowship with other Christians, we don't have to deal with burdens and persecution by ourselves. We have a community of people who know us and love us and will shoulder the bad times with us. God created us to be relational beings—which is why fellowship is so critical to every Christian.

Reflections

Service

Daniel 3:17
"If it be so, our God whom we serve is able to deliver us from the furnace of blazing fire."

Week Thirty-One   **Day Seven**

This is the infamous story of Daniel's three pals being tossed in the fiery furnace. What happened was...Nebuchadnezzar builds this big image and makes everyone worship it. However, the three Hebrew boys decline the king's demand. So, Nebuchadnezzar, enraged, has the boys tied up and thrown into the fiery furnace. Not before, however they told the king that they didn't know what God would do but nevertheless they were not going to bow down to an idol.

Wow! Certainly don't know if I could do that, astonishing. These heroes of the faith did not focus on a result demanded from God, they just served Him as instructed. They tell this demanding human that their God is able, "if it be so" to reward them with life for serving just Him. Why would they bow down to any other god, certainly the idol couldn't offer a deal as good as that? Why would they, indeed. Why would we?

Reflections

Worship

Ezekiel 34:22
"I will deliver my flock and they will no longer be a prey; I will judge between the fat sheep and the lean sheep."

Week Thirty-Two   **Day One**

Life is just not fair! Bad things happen to good people! It seems like the evil of the world is winning the race. Why is it so hard, in that, as I try to do the right thing there always seems to be a challenge to doing so? On the other hand, the evil of the world seems to have an easy broad highway to navigate on. I wrote a book called "Behind the Glass," which explains how bad things happen to good people. I try to unpack some of these questions, I would love for you to read it and give some feedback.

We worship God because He is the Good Shepherd. Ezekiel in this chapter and the one before it is comparing good shepherds with the false shepherds. Ultimately, we know God is the Good Shepherd but also in this world today there are good ones and bad ones. There are spiritual leaders of people who are doing right and wrong things. To break down even further, there are good and bad sheep. There are flock members, people who profess to be believers, Christians who are good and bad, who are authentic and who are false.

However unfair the world seems, God has control. The bad are not actually getting away with anything. The good are being recognized by Him. There will be a sorting out in due time. There is eternal punishment for those who are not truly believers in God and His Son. Stay strong good sheep, we have a Shepherd who knows us and He is worthy of our worship.

Reflections

Bible Reading

Esther 5:2
"Esther the queen…obtained favor…so Esther came near…
and the king said what is troubling you…"

Week Thirty-Two   **Day Two**

Growing up kids seek approval from those around them. They want to be complimented on their efforts to conform to the family norms and lifted up when they excel. In my family just doing the norm or meeting the minimal standard never brought any recognition. However, when I excelled in a sport, academics or even in some sort of personal development my parents made sure that they let me know they recognized the efforts. Usually these were not great achievements but efforts beyond my normal behaviors were met with appreciation.

God does the same thing with us. When we do as He instructs, we find favor with Him. He puts us in positions to be influential, be heard, to make a difference or just be a good example. In Esther 5:2, the author tells us that "it happened when the king saw Esther the queen standing in the court, she obtained favor in his sight…" God was enabling Esther to be in a position of favor before the king so she could be instrumental in saving the lives of the Israelites captive in Babylon. God's Word gives us what we need to have for God to find favor in us. He clearly wants to reward our good behavior and allow us to be useful in His mission to save this lost and dying world.

Reflections

Prayer

Acts 7:55
"Being full of the Holy Spirit he gazed intently into heaven and saw the glory of God, and Jesus standing at the right hand of God…"

Week Thirty-Two   **Day Three**

The Bible is full of accounts of folks who in their prayer time were able to see into the throne room of God. Call them visions, dreams or out of body experiences, whatever. They all happened in a time of their prayer discipline. These events would make a good Bible study, hey, even a good book.

Today, Luke is relating one of those events. Stephen is actually about to be stoned to death for his Christian beliefs. What he told the religious leaders struck such a chord of truth about their lives they could not stand it. They dragged him right out from their hearing and stoned him.

Even as rocks were being hurled at him Stephen prayed to God. God gave him a glimpse of the glory that would soon surround him. God also gave Him peace in this horrible situation. Stephen was so full of peace that he even ask God to forgive the men doing this and he peacefully died.

Prayer works. I must to admit I have never faced stoning but I have faced an unfair accusation, a trial and then spent time in prison for something I did not do. Not nearly as holy as Stephen, but I can say prayer works.

Reflections

Meditation

Judges 2:2
"You shall make no covenant with the inhabitants of this land…but you have not obeyed Me; what is this that you have done?"

Week Thirty-Two   **Day Four**

When I was in prison, I had a prescription for ibuprofen. It came on a card and you would punch each tablet out as needed. At the end of the month you turn the card in and they would give you a new thirty day supply. Having extra at the end of the month I punched them all out, five or six and turned the card in for a new one. There was a major shake down and the loose pills were in my locker and I got in trouble. I told the mediator I had no clue about the rule. They were issued to me and were not illegal drugs or ones obtained from someone else. I still got written up and sanctioned for loose medicines.

If you do not know the rules it is tough to follow them. The writer of Judges is telling the people of God they have no excuse. They had a covenant with God and have broken it. They were fully aware of what God expected and still were disobedient.

Meditation is the answer. God will tell you what He expects and how He expects you to achieve His goals. We are without excuse because we have free access to God. It is important to know, unlike me in prison, we actually have no excuses before God.

Reflections

Physical Wellness

Titus 2:12
"Instructing us to deny ungodliness and worldly desires and to live sensibly, righteously, and godly in the present age..."

Week Thirty-Two   **Day Five**

Today folks have an overpowering attraction for the secular world. Christians or not, this is a true statement. God knows we are sinners and will continue to sin. He knows that the world is attractive to us and that the evil one makes it hard to resist his ways.

That is why spiritual disciplines are so important. They are our protection against the wiles of the devil. If we form good habits in our spiritual journey, we will not be apt to fall for the lures of the world. God allows Satan to lurk around and try to draw us away from God's directions.

Paul is writing to one of his trainees, Titus. He wants him to tell his congregation to be aware of what the evil one is doing. We must stay alert and assume that the Evil One will always try to take a run at us. He wants us to stumble and fall.

Physical wellness is important. There are times when we are apt to give in to the world, when we are ill, out of shape, stuck in self-pity and self-indulgence. Stop it right now! Start self-care and slowly work yourself into a posture of physical readiness. Do not be a notch on Satan's belt.

Reflections

Fellowship

Philemon 1:20
"Yes, brother, let me benefit from you in the Lord;
refreshing my heart in Christ."

Week Thirty-Two   **Day Six**

One of the reasons fellowship is so important is that you can begin to surround yourself with folks you can count on. The world is full of selfish and self-centered people, folks who only want to meet their own needs, with no regard for anyone else.

This is true of all of us from time to time. A friend called this morning and wanted a ride to a twelve step meeting instead of walking in the rain. I missed the call and was saddened that I missed the opportunity to help him out. I was all ready and had no reason not to go the two miles out of my way to pick him up.

Paul is writing to a brother in the faith. He is asking him for a favor. He knows that he could demand compliance because of his apostleship. He does not, as a fellowship member he just asks nicely.

He tells Philemon he knows that he will comply because they are brothers in the faith. The fellowship helps those in the group who need it. That is how God dispenses His blessings. I do not like asking for help but when I refuse to then I deny someone else the blessing God wanted for them.

Reflections

Service

Ezekiel 22:30
"I searched for a man among them who should build up the wall and stand in the gap before Me...but I found no one."

Week Thirty-Two   **Day Seven**

Years ago, there was a movement called Promise Keepers. I did not agree with everything they stood for. There was one outstanding concept of theirs that I supported whole heartedly, that was the idea of standing in the gap.

The call was for men to stand up and be what God intended them to be. Good fathers, husbands, employees and employers. Be the kind of men that will stand in the gap by doing the hard right thing. God needs men of faith to accomplish His mission on earth.

Here, Ezekiel is stating that there are plenty of folks around to do the job. Why is it not getting done? He points out in the verse before this one that there are various groups in Israel's society that are sinning, being disobedient to God. What God needs is for them to correct their ways and begin to stand in the gap. Stand up and begin to serve God by serving the people of God. Get the jobs done that need to be accomplished.

I'm not beating anyone up here, although I believe Ezekiel was. The thing that makes us different from the folks following the world's chaos is our service to one another. How many blessings have we missed because we were not looking for the opportunity to serve?

Reflections

Worship

Daniel 2:47
"Surely your God is a God of gods and a Lord of kings..."

Week Thirty-Three   **Day One**

I let this woman with only a couple of items in front of me at the check-out. You would have thought I handed her a gazillion dollars and a housekeeper! She gushed and thanked me, *profusely*. So, my sneaky Holy Spirt lays this on me: do you make that big of a production when thanking God for what He's done for you? Ouch.

Worship is giving value to something or someone. Do we value God? If we do, why aren't we more over-the-top with our worship of and to Him? Let's try to remember how mighty our God is, how merciful He is, how all-encompassing His love is for us. Let's remember to tell Him how much we worship Him.

Reflections

Bible Reading

Nehemiah 13:14
"Remember me for this, O my God, and do not blot out
my loyal deeds which I have performed for the house of
my God."

Week Thirty-Three   **Day Two**

Nobody in their right minds chooses to be a Pastor! You can choose to be a race car driver, an underwater welder or an astronaut, but you do not choose to become a Pastor. Becoming a Pastor has to be a calling from God or else there is nothing but misery and pain that lies ahead. As a Pastor you always hear, "Not what have you done for me, but what have you done for me lately?" It just seems like there is a lot of giving, forgiving, accepting and comforting. Yet, when a Pastor needs something, gets tired or shows signs of weakness folks are surprised and doubt their faith.

Nehemiah, the wonderful post-exile leader of the Israelites, knew exactly what I am talking about. In Nehemiah 13:14, he asked God to, "Remember me for this, O my God, and do not blot out my loyal deeds which I have performed for the house of my God and its services." Today we would call that self-serving; Nehemiah, however, understands how quick people forget and seek support and confirmation for God, who never forgets or fails to recognize work being done on His behalf. God's Word is full of examples that help us understand how truly interested God is in our well-being. Great news!

Reflections

Prayer

Job 16:17
"Although there is no violence in my hands
and my prayer is pure."

Week Thirty-Three   **Day Three**

Prayer is pure. What does that mean? First of all, prayer that is not pure cannot be heard by God. Because of God's perfectness, anything that has an ounce of sin attached is not going to get through. So, what makes a prayer pure? A couple of things: first, prayer must come from the heart - God can see past our ulterior motives and is actually only interested in what our heart yearns for and that which aligns with His will. Secondly, we ourselves must be pure – we need to confess our sins to God, asking heartfelt forgiveness. Of course, our prayers aren't pure if we don't know and trust God, which means, we have to trust that God will answer our prayers in ways that are pleasing to Him and His will. Lastly, we must come with a thankful heart; we have to acknowledge all the wonderful things He has done and prayers that He has answered.

Reflections

Meditation

Matthew 7:26
"Everyone who hears these words of Mine and does not act
upon them, will be like a foolish man who
built his house on the sand."

Week Thirty-Three   **Day Four**

What a wonderful verse to meditate upon! When we meditate, we are conversing with God. This is an intimate God and you time. He wants to hear what you have to say and He expects us to listen to what He has to say and act upon it. I can't tell you how many times I've pleaded with God about something, He answers in a way I'm not thrilled about and I then convince myself it wasn't God talking. Yep, my house is on the sand.

This is a foundational thing. Houses built on the sand don't last. Houses built on rock do. Being able to go forward and complete an assignment for God is very foundational – it builds a firm base for our relationship with God, a foundation built on trust. If we can't listen to God and *act*, we're not getting it.

Reflections

Physical Wellness

2 Timothy 1:14
"Guard, through the Holy Spirit who dwells in us,
the treasure which has been entrusted to you."

Week Thirty-Three   **Day Five**

Why is it that we really clean and spruce up our homes before guests come? Why do we get rid of all the dust and dirt and clutter? Why do we put out flowers and our good china? Because we want to provide the best for our guest. We want them to feel comfortable in a clean and clutter less home.

It brings me to my knees when I think of the dust and dirt and clutter in my body – the house of the Holy Spirit. It is gross! We must remember that the Holy Spirit – GOD! – lives in our hearts – that's the only place. We must get rid of all the dust and dirt and clutter, all the poisons and chaos. We must honor the home of God. For each of us this may mean different things (I may need to quit smoking, you may need to eliminate alcohol), but we all need to be aware of what accommodations we provide for our treasure!

Reflections

Fellowship

Proverbs 18:24
"A man of too many friends comes to ruin, but there is a friend who sticks closer than a brother."

Week Thirty-Three   **Day Six**

This is another sound axiom. Yes, we are to fellowship with one another, but having – and, more importantly, being – "a friend who sticks closer than a brother" is just as important. I'm lucky in that I have brothers who always have my back – not all of us do – but I also have a friend or two that knows where the "bodies are hidden." These are the gals I've written about who keep me honest and growing and always feeling loved. One "person-ship" in particular of mine makes me think about the relationship I have with Jesus. It is so pure and non-judgmental and so full of love and laughter; she does not give a hoot about much that I do or say, she just simply wants to be with me and I, her. I absolutely adore who I am when I am with this person! My relationship with Jesus is like that times a gazillion trillion. The folks that become our "people" might be angels!

Reflections

Service

Ephesians 6:6
"Not by the way of eyeservice, as men-pleasers, but as slaves
of Christ, doing the will of God from the heart."

Week Thirty-Three   **Day Seven**

Service, as this verse points out, must be from the heart. What
does that even mean? Well, there has been a time or two that I
volunteered to, say, serve the homeless during a holiday. On the
day of, I woke up with the attitude of an ungrateful adolescent
who's being made to do a chore. That, my friends, is service *not
from the heart*. Jesus delighted in helping others; He lived for
it. For us to be like Jesus, we must adopt this same delighted
attitude in our dealings with others.

Reflections

Worship

Mark 3:29
"Whoever blasphemes against the Holy Spirit never has
forgiveness, but is guilty of an eternal sin…"

Week Thirty-Four   **Day One**

So, the rumor is that suicide is the unpardonable sin. I've
heard that all my life. I do not think my parents subscribed to
that theory but I heard it growing up in the church. I did not
think much about the concept until I went to seminary and
became a Pastor.

It was as a Pastor in a rural southern Virginia county that
I began to run across that exact question. Often folks would
pontificate about their knowledge of God and they would state
that suicide is the unpardonable sin. These were well-meaning,
raised-in-the- church folks displaying a grave misconception.

Mark tells us plainly that there will be no forgiveness if
you blaspheme the Holy Spirit. He mentions nothing about
suicide. He is telling us just not giving God the credit He is
due, that is blasphemous and unforgivable. We worship God
because He will forgive us our sins and allow us to get back
into the correct posture before Him. He will forgive anything
we do; however, He will not forgive giving credit to other
people, places or things for His work. In the Book of Exodus,
God tells Moses that Pharaoh has a hard heart, that is the basis
of blasphemy.

Reflections

Bible Reading

Ezra 8:22
"The hand of God is favorably disposed to all those who seek Him, but His power and His anger are against all those who forsake Him."

Week Thirty-Four   **Day Two**

Look around your circles of influence today. Really take a gander at the folks you come in contact with. Do they look, act, appear to be folks secure in their life? Do they smile, laugh, seek pleasure in the little things? Or are they short, ill at ease with the world and refuse to see the "glass half full?" Folks that feel alone in this world, those who feel they are rolling a rock uphill all the time, feel unprotected from the forces that want to oppress them, are truly to be pitied.

God wants us to know that He is there to protect us and that He has a plan for our life. We do not have to feel alone. Ezra, another of the post-exile prophets, understood this. When it came time to lead a group of refugee Israelites out of Babylon and back to Jerusalem, he knew he could count on God. In Ezra 8:22, he tells his fellow travelers, "the hand of God is favorably disposed to all those who seek Him…" Ezra knew the going was going to be tough but did not want to depend upon his captors to provide safe passage, he knew God alone was all he needed. The same goes for us today, those who believe are protected and provided for by God.

Reflections

Prayer

Esther 4:14
"For if you remain silent at this time, relief and deliverance
will arise for the Jews from another place…"

Week Thirty-Four   **Day Three**

We were talking the other day at a twelve step meeting I was at about a blind alley. It's a place that you can get yourself into that has no way out, or maybe you find yourself there through no fault of your own. Regardless of how you get there the situation seems hopeless. Our addictions can get us there, no matter what they are.

I had to reflect on that blind alley for a day or two. I came to understand that I had actually never been in one. I had been in some dumb places, places where morality and good manners were not a must. I had been in places where judges, police and correctional officers ran my life, but no blind alleys.

There has always been a way out for me. At times the options were severely limited. At times the consequences of my actions made getting out painful and rigorous. Yet, there was always a way out. I give all the credit to God.

Esther is being told by her cousin Mordecai that God was going to provide a way for their people. If not through her position as queen somehow, He would make it happen. God always has a way to care for those who believe in Him.

Prayer gives us that way out. When we can contact the Power greater than ourselves, He will provide the way. We need to just be willing to accept the consequences for our actions and humbly understand God is in control.

Reflections

Meditation

Luke 6:46
"Why do you call me Lord, Lord and do not what I say?"

Week Thirty-Four   **Day Four**

Life is hard. It is even harder when you feel like the rules of society do not apply to you. My Dad was always telling me that there were rules for a reason. They were to keep me safe, help me live alongside other humans or just to keep me on the correct moral path. As a kid you just say, "yes sir," then go out and play.

As I got older, I began to realize rules were no joke. The violation of normal societal morays could bring serious consequences. It did not matter if everyone was doing it, wrong is wrong and there are no excuses.

Dr. Luke is giving his version of the Sermon on the Mount, a wonderful discourse by Jesus. In theological terms it is Jesus' systematic theology. The compilation of His teaching is systematically building one concept on another for the purpose of getting to the correct posture before God.

Toward the end Jesus says, "Why do you call me Lord? You call me Lord but do not follow my instructions." My Dad would tell me the exact same thing, without the Lord part, of course. If we would take the time to meditate on how well our own ideas, plans and actions work out we will find they fall very short compared to God's plan. Worst of all is when we do finally realize how limited we really are and could have avoided a lot of pain in our life if we would have just listened to God.

Reflections

Physical Wellness

Zechariah 3:4
"I have taken your iniquity away from you and will clothe
you with festal robes."

Week Thirty-Four   **Day Five**

Joshua the high priest is cleansed in this vision. He had been
charged with being unfit to serve in this office. This is also a
picture of the restoration of the nation of Israel before God.
Of great importance to us today is its prophetic significance,
illustrating the future cleaning of the nation and us as believers
at the return of Jesus.

We are considered as being clothed in filthy rags. Satan
wants us to believe that we are too filthy and degenerate for
God to care for us. He accuses us before God as being not
worthy of His love. He wants us to believe that we have no
other choice but to follow the way of the world into hell.

God says He has taken away our sins with the death of
Jesus on the cross. We can be dressed in fine clothes, cleansed
and acceptable before Him. At this point these are visons and
prophesies of encouragement the prophet is relating to the
congregation.

The Good News is that no matter what you have done or
the depths or distance you have put between yourself and God
makes no difference. We can get right today. With the help
of the Holy Spirt, we can get our self spiritually, mentally and
physically well to be of use to God.

Reflections

Fellowship

Acts 2:42
"They were continually devoting themselves to the apostle's teaching and to fellowship to the breaking of bread and prayer."

Week Thirty-Four   **Day Six**

There is nothing like going through a tough time with a group of people and getting to the other side. I remember when I graduated from The Citadel, a military college, Jump School, Air Assault school, Flight School and got my doctorate. There were bonds cemented with the folks I faced these challenges with. These are ties that bind us together, even today, many years after the successful completions of the rigorous training.

Being like-minded with others is hard to find in today's society. Folks do not struggle together. We are all individuals demanding our own way. We do not lean on each other because the world says we are weak if we need help.

Dr. Luke says that after the Pentecost event, the indwelling of the Holy Spirit on the believers, these folks bonded like never before. A fellowship was created that brought believers closer together, sharing with each other the burdens of life.

What a great picture he paints. It is exactly what God had in mind as He planned to let us humans spread His message. God is never intending us to do it alone, and always wants us to join forces with each other to make this journey called the Christian life.

Reflections

Service

Lamentations 1:9
"She did not consider her future; therefore, she has fallen astonishingly; she has no comforter. See, O Lord, my affliction, for the enemy has magnified himself!"

Week Thirty-Four   **Day Seven**

Have you ever felt like this? Through your own actions you come to a place where you are alone. The wolf is at the door, and like the three little pigs story, he is getting ready to blow your house down. There is no one on the horizon to help you make your life straight. Everyone has abandoned you. You are truly alone.

Jeremiah is prophesizing the desolation of Jerusalem. Through their own disobedience they are being dealt with severely by God. He has had enough and it is now time to pay the consequences for their actions. God is not pleased and they have no excuse to offer.

My belief is we have all been there. That is why service is so important. God wants to send help, if only we would go. He wants to provide a comforter but who is willing to serve another? It is no mystery about how we get to these places in our lives. It is also no mystery that God is not going to give up on us. Punishment or not, He wants us to get the message of His love for us. He has sent a comforter in the Holy Spirit. He will also send help in the form of a servant willing to be obedient. Is He asking you to go to serve someone today?

Reflections

Worship

Mark 9:23b
"All things are possible to him who believes…"

Week Thirty-Five   **Day One**

What exactly *does* worship look like? How do we worship? I think we'll all agree that singing, raising our hands, even shouting to the Lord in praise are aspects of worship. But what about the rest of the week? How do we worship God in the day-to-day activities that define our lives? First of all, following the spiritual disciplines outlined in Charlie's book, *When Life Shows Up;* and, obviously, these are the topics for our weekly devotions; are forms of worship. Worship is simply showing, to our God, our faith and love and loyalty.

My favorite place in the world to worship is outside, in my garden. I always feel the presence of Jesus. Always. And I rejoice in it. It makes my heart so happy and my soul so fulfilled. And I guess what I mean by worshipping in the garden is I simply let the Holy Spirit guide my thoughts – which always brings me to the awesomeness of the Master Gardener. We can worship God while doing the laundry, or in the grocery store by offering a big ol' smile to a stranger (or, because we're a masked society now, a gentle nod of acknowledgement). The point is, every second of our lives can be spent in worship – individually and corporately; in fact, I'll be so bold to say every second of our lives *should* be spent in worship!

Reflections

Bible Reading

2 Kings 7:1
"Elisha said, 'Listen to the Word of the Lord…behold you shall see it with your own eyes…'"

Week Thirty-Five   **Day Two**

Would it not be nice to have a crystal ball to be able to see into the future? You could always know what's going to happen before it *actually* happens - what great insight that would be. No more floundering around wondering if you have made the correct choice. No more agonizing decisions, making dramas. Just simple, clear cut, intelligent data supplied by the crystal ball and bam, a good decision. We all know that is not even in the realm of possibility. Even if it was, we humans would find a way to pervert it for profit and the genie who gave it to us would end up taking it away.

Yet, actually the Bible is full of insight about what our tomorrows will be. God routinely told his prophets what to expect both in the immediate future and the distant. In 2 Kings 7:1 God lets Elisha know what is going to happen the very next day. Elisha says, "Listen to the word of the Lord, tomorrow at this time…" The Israelites were under siege and running out of food, God, though Elisha, let them know He was about ready to solve that problem. God is telling us as well what we need to know so that we will be ready for our tomorrows. We have to study His Word so that we can begin to recognize His language and ways of communicating with us.

Reflections

Prayer

Nehemiah 6:16
"When all...the nations surrounding us saw...they recognized this had been accomplished with the help of our God."

Prayer is an amazing privilege - a privilege selflessly given to us through Jesus dying on the cross for our sins. And, for me, it is extremely intimate. It is one of the reasons I'm not big fan of praying out loud in a group. God knows our hearts; He knows stuff about us that we may not always be aware of. When I go to Him in prayer, I lay it all out, but what happens when I don't know what to pray?

There are times when I am so angry, or hurting so badly, or my thoughts are so chaotic, that I can't find the words to go to God with; that's when the Holy Spirit swoops in and intercedes. Romans 8:26 tells us, "the Spirit helps us in our weakness. We do not know what we ought to pray for, but the Spirit himself intercedes for us with groans that words cannot express." I love that! "Groan[ings] that words cannot express". Friends, I don't know how it all works, but what I do know is that God hears those groans. So, when you are "stuck", please be comforted by knowing the Holy Spirit has your back!

Reflections

Meditation

John 3:27
"A man can receive nothing,
unless it has been given from heaven…"

Week Thirty-FiveDay Four

The whole purpose of meditation is resting with God and focusing on tuning into the heart of God. What happens when that focus is waning or constantly being interrupted by the wandering thoughts in our heads? I think it is safe to say that all of us struggle to stay focused and in the contemplative state that is so necessary for meditation. It is so easy to let the "noise" distract us from our true purpose: focusing on God.

I find that Psalms 139:23-24 gives me the opportunity to ask God to walk me through these pesky interruptions: "Search me, God, and know my heart; test me and know my anxious thoughts. See if there is any offensive way in me and lead me in the way everlasting." In fact, I find the only way to combat a noisy mind is to spend time in quiet contemplation, letting God walk me through all the mess stored in my little brain. As I continue this meditative practice, my knowledge of God broadens and my relationship with Him deepens.

Reflections

Physical Wellness

Zephaniah 3:17

"The Lord God is in your midst, a victorious warrior..."

Week Thirty-Five   **Day Five**

What, exactly, does physical wellness look like? Do I need to have a six pack to qualify? Should I be able to lift the equivalent of my own body weight? Do I give up my B&R mint chocolate chip ice cream? Not necessarily. Physical wellness is more of a mindset than anything else.

This may mean different things for different people. I may struggle with using food to comfort myself as a substitute for letting God comfort me; for you, it may be a margarita. Conversely, I don't mean to say that if you smoke cigarettes, you don't have a relationship with God. What I am trying to say is, when we view our physical selves as holy temples for God and act accordingly, we are practicing the spiritual discipline of physical wellness.

Reflections

Fellowship

Romans 8:31
"If God is for us, who is against us?"

Week Thirty-Five   **Day Six**

What a fellowship, what a joy divine,
Leaning on the everlasting arms.
What a blessedness, what a peace is mine,
Leaning on the everlasting arms.
Leaning, leaning,
Safe and secure from all alarms.
Leaning, leaning,
Leaning on the everlasting arms.
- Iris DeMent

This song reminds me of Wednesday night prayer meetings. It reminds me of our Scripture today: really, if God *is* for us, who cares who's against us? What an amazing concept! To carry that thought further, when we have the Lord God Almighty on our side, what else do we need? When I meditate on that belief, I truly do find comfort and a peacefulness in my heart.

The next time you are facing something troublesome and that horrible terror overwhelms you, recite this verse – over and over. And really let the notion that the Creator of everything, the Ruler of forever, totally has your back and is so incredibly in love with you.

Reflections

Service

Genesis 4:9b
"Am I my brother's keeper?"

Week Thirty-Five   **Day Seven**

The answer to that is, yes. Part of our Christian service is to uplift one another, to share burdens, to hold accountable. And when it comes to family, it isn't always easy. Same can be said for fellow brothers and sisters in Christ – not always easy. Just like family, we don't always get to pick those who are in the Christianity thing with us. Like it or not, we are responsible for them. And they for us.

Tending to people who are hurting and keeping our "brothers" on the right track isn't just for the leaders in our churches. Galatians 5:13 commands us to "...through love serve one another." It isn't always easy, that's for sure. Sometimes I find it easier to minister to a homeless person than it is to help a fellow Christian who has come on hard times and is struggling just to, say, pay bills. So, as we walk this path we're on, let's try to be especially mindful of what we can do to help our family in Christ.

Reflections

Worship

1 Corinthians 1:28
"The base things of the world and despised, God has chosen, the things that are not, that He might nullify the things that are; that no man should boast before God."

Week Thirty-Six   **Day One**

Throughout the Bible there has been a common misconception. In fact, today that same faulty thinking exists. It is erroneous to believe that if you are rich, life is good for you and you are in good health, it is because God is showing favor to you. Conversely, if you are down on your luck, with few resources and sickly, you must have sinned so God is punishing you.

This was something Jesus had to face in His ministry. Even His disciples could not believe that it was actually hard for a rich man to get into heaven. They figure if they cannot, who can? Nevertheless, this shallow thinking still persists today.

Paul wants the folks at Corinth to understand that dynamic is wrong. In fact, it is completely opposite. God uses the base and despised folks of this world to accomplish His goals. I wrote a book about this subject entitled, "Labels."

We worship a God who sees us for who we are. We are naked before Him, without skin color, money, possessions, power or sex. We are blank slates He can use to write a story with. Praise God, for we who have been labeled can still be used in a powerful way by God.

Reflections

Bible Reading

1 Kings 22:14
"Micaiah said, 'As the Lord lives, what the Lord says to me,
that I will speak.'"

Week Thirty-Six   **Day Two**

Sometimes it is tough to hear what others have to say. We do not like their tone, their delivery or the fact that often they seem to be the bearer of bad tidings. Sometimes we just do not like the messenger and refuse to listen no matter what comes out of their mouths. The problem with that is we narrow down and drastically reduce possible pertinent data that we need to make intelligent decisions. If we always "shoot the messenger," we will constantly place our self behind the information power curve.

King Ahab did not like the prophet of God that worked in the Israelites country. Ahab did not like asking him for guidance because he seemed to always have a message from God that he did not want to hear. As a result, he was willing to march ahead without prophetic information or even allowed his "yes" men to tell him what he wanted to hear. In 1 Kings 22:14, when the prophet of God was asked to go along with the "yes" men of the king he said, "As the Lord lives, what the Lord says to me, that I will speak." God's Word is true, pulls no punches and bears no allegiance to any man. If we want truth and an accurate assessment of where we are before God, His Word is there for us.

Reflections

Prayer

Hebrews 10:24
"Let us consider how to stimulate one another
to love and good deeds…"

Week Thirty-Six   **Day Three**

As an Army officer I was tasked often to stimulate, encourage, motivate and drive forward men in my unit. I had to learn to lead them to a place in their personal development so they could be promoted and be a valuable part of a functioning unit.

While I was in, gone were the days of the ranting and raving chain of command. Yelling and berating folks never has a lasting leadership potential. Leading not pushing was my way of doing things. Relational leadership is what they call it today.

The writer of Hebrews is encouraging the fellowship of believers to do just that. Help each other find ways to be productive members of the congregation. Stimulate each other to personal growth and in their own spiritual walk. We need to teach each other God's ways and how to best serve Him.

Prayer is the best tool for that, not a whip or verbal abuse. Praying for each other's edification in the ways of God. We may not know how to motivate someone in a way that works for them but God does. He will help us help them. Prayer puts us in contact with God and we gain great insight on how to help those God puts in our sphere of influence.

Reflections

Meditation

1 Peter 3:15
"Sanctify Christ as Lord in your hearts, always being ready
to make a defense to everyone who asks you to give an
account for the hope that is in you..."

Week Thirty-Six   **Day Four**

It has always amazed me that I can remember the facts and
figures of my favorite football team but cannot remember
someone's name or phone number. My smart phone busted
about a year ago and I was lost. I had no one's phone number
in my head. If it had not been for the technicians at the store,
I would never have recovered all those numbers.

Some of my memory issues comes from not paying
attention. Some comes from not caring enough to make any
effort to remember. Some of it comes from the limits of my
human abilities. Once again, it seems I can remember the
things I am interested in.

Peter wants us to know that it is important to know what
you believe in. Not only know it but be able to explain to
others. Our job as Christians, is to spread the Good News of
Jesus' saving death on the cross.

Meditation on these subjects gets us there. We have to
think about what God is saying to us. How does His Word
apply to us? Where do I fit into His plan? These things are
important and it is through time spent with God in meditation
that we begin to grasp the answers.

Reflections

Physical Wellness

Judges 15:14
"The Spirit of the Lord came up him mightily so that the
ropes that were on his arms
were as flax that is burned with fire..."

Week Thirty-Six   **Day Five**

The story of Samson has always been one that I enjoyed. Samson was like a real life superhero. He had great strength and a great mission. His job was to help free his people from the rule of a dominating nation. God gave him a specific gift to accomplish it with, strength and courage.

It is sad when you see someone with so much potential and talent not living up to expectations. I know putting expectations on others is dangerous. We do, however, always want to see folks live up to their fullest potential. When they do not it just seems like a waste.

These events happened before Samson began to disregard his calling. He broke these bonds and killed a thousand of the enemy forces with the jawbone of a donkey, superhero, right? What a fantastic feat!

We are all given abilities by God to accomplish His mission here on earth. How often do we fail to use them for His purpose? We do not stay physically well enough to keep these abilities honed. We get lazy and lose interest. God has big plans for us and we so often just get lethargic and become not just unmotivated but not useful. Get fit, stay prepared to accomplish the superhero feats God has for you.

Reflections

Fellowship

Exodus 12:36
"The Lord has given the people favor in the sight of the
Egyptians, so they let them have their request. Thus, they
plundered the Egyptians."

Week Thirty-Six   **Day Six**

This is the part of the Exodus story that happens right after
God struck down all the first born of the children and animals
of the Egyptian people. What an awful time for those folks.
Their leader was so hard-hearted that he would not free
God's people. Now this final plague of ten was the last straw.
Everyone in the country has suffered a loss, even Pharaoh.

God's people now went to the Egyptian families and asked
for their valuables. The Egyptians were so ready to get rid of
the Israelites they gave them what they wanted, an amazing
event for sure.

God's people had to act as a fellowship, be obedient for
this phase of the exodus to happen. The whole group had to
get themselves ready, prepare the Passover meal and put the
blood of a sacrificial animal over their doorways. The group as
a whole functioned in one accord to be in the correct posture
before God to accomplish this great feat. God can use us to
accomplish just as great feats if we will act as one, if we as a
fellowship of believers will act as one and be obedient.

Reflections

Service

Mark 2:4
"Being unable to get to Him because of the crowd, they removed the roof above Him; and when they had dug an opening, let down the pallet on which the paralytic was lying."

Week Thirty-Six   **Day Seven**

What great friends this guy had. Do you have the kind of friends who would go to any length to see that your needs are met? Are you the kind of servant that would go to any lengths to help out someone else? The only way I can answer these questions is, "I sure hope so!"

Jesus is teaching and healing the sick. The crowd was so dense the friends could not get their buddy close to Him. They went the extra mile, not wanting to fail their buddy and came up with a plan. What a great reminder to me of how important my calling as a servant is. I might be called to be the only answer someone else has to solve their dilemma. I might be used in such a powerful way someone else's life may be changed forever.

I want to be that kind of servant. I know God will use me in small ways to get me trained up. I have to be purposeful in seeking opportunities to serve. I have to be available to others. I have to be known as the kind of guy who is glad to help. I also have be the kind of servant that will not give up.

Reflections

Worship

Ephesians 3:20
"Now to Him who is able to do far more abundantly than all that we ask or think, according to the power at work within us."

Week Thirty-Seven   **Day One**

This passage is a prayer from Paul on the behalf of the Ephesian Christians. I want you to notice this particular part: "...far more abundantly than all that we ask or think..." Paul is telling all of us here that we are to come to God with everything. We ask for a scoop of ice cream and He gives us a blown-out banana Sundae split – with extra whipped cream and cherries!

When we are worshipping God, individually or collectively, let's remember to acknowledge His "abundanceness". Let's thank Him for how He treats us like royalty. Let's humbly, with awe, bask in His love.

Reflections

Bible Reading

2 Timothy 2:15
"Be diligent to present yourself approved...handling
accurately the Word of truth."

Week Thirty-Seven   **Day Two**

Growing up my parents used to always say to me, "If you're going to do something, you need to do it right!" They were correct; it does not make sense to do things halfway. If you run around doing things halfway it leads to a life full of "half stuff." What good is a life that is littered with half of everything? Nothing completed, nothing really done well, nothing to hold up as complete. It is easy to do and it may not be the outcome you really want. Yet, when you start down the path of half measures it just seems to get ingrained.

The Bible teaches us that we need to do all that we attempt to the best of our ability. The Apostle Paul in his letter to his protégé Timothy offers some advice along that line. In 2 Timothy 2:15, he tells Timothy to, "Be diligent to present yourself approved to God as a workman who does not need to be ashamed, handling accurately the Word of truth..." It is our duty as Christians to learn, grow and to correctly apply God's Word to our life. We need to walk in a way that demonstrates these traits to those around us, no half measures.

Reflections

Prayer

Acts 2:42
"They were continually devoting themselves to the apostles'
teaching and to fellowship,
to the breaking of bread and to prayer."

Week Thirty-Seven   **Day Three**

Broadly, this passage is talking about the three thousand or so souls that accepted Jesus Christ as their Lord and Savior and were baptized. Luke tells us that these new Christians devoted themselves to the apostles' teachings, fellowshipping among one another, celebrating the Lord's supper and to prayer. Do we devote ourselves to any of that?

Incidentally, the Greek word used here indicates plural for prayer. That means that all sorts of prayers were offered up. I bet there were prayers of thanksgiving, hope, asking for forgiveness and grace. The point is prayer is important – new Christian or veteran. In fact, let's try to *devote* ourselves to having conversations with Jesus.

Reflections

Meditation

Genesis 12:4
"So Abram went forth as the Lord had spoken to him..."

Week Thirty-Seven   **Day Four**

I love to garden. I love getting dirt crammed up under my fingernails. I love feeling the sun. I love watching things I planted produce flowers and vegetables. It's all so amazing! But my absolute, all-time favorite thing about gardening is that's where I feel the presence of God the most – gardening with Jesus, is what I call it. The majority of the time, I "pretend" Jesus is kneeling right beside me, just yakkety yakking away. And He does!!! Sometimes my heart is moved to just be in awe of all the clever creatures and plants He's given us. Other times, the Holy Spirit brings up something that needs attention.

This is what meditation can look like in my life. And it is all because "I showed up". Of course, there are many, many times during a gardening session that I have to consciously bring my thoughts back (usually because they've landed on some ick I shouldn't be thinking about). And God really does talk to me. It is one of the sweetest times during my day.

Reflections

Physical Wellness

Week Thirty-Seven　　　　　　　　　　　　　　**Day Five**

I feel led to venture off-course today, sorta. So many of us have had less-than-stellar backgrounds; so many of us are not kind to our bodies because of shame or addiction or having been bullied or simply bad life choices; so many of us self-harm our bodies to mask the pain our souls feel. Your past does not matter to Jesus. At all. He loves us no matter what has happened in our past. He wants to wrap His loving arms around us and comfort all the physical – and mental and emotional – pain we endure.

You would think with all the talk in Scripture about our souls that God wasn't really interested in our physical wellness. In fact, there are countless examples in the Bible that show us God did not ease the physical burdens of some people (think Paul and his unspecified affliction). But God does. He cares so much that He knows how many hairs are on our head. You know He knows how many cells and flakes of skin each one of us has.

I say all that to say this: regardless of your past physical wellbeing or how you have treated your body up to this point, please know that Jesus is rooting for you - He so cares and loves us. And He encourages us to take care of our physical being because it is important to Him. You are worth taking care of yourself. Period.

Reflections

Fellowship

Philippians 2:25
"I thought it necessary to send to you Epaphroditus, my brother and fellow worker and fellow soldier, who is also your messenger and minister to my need."

Week Thirty-Seven   **Day Six**

Paul's letter to the Philippians was delivered by Epaphroditus. In it, Paul gives him five titles: brother, worker, soldier, messenger, and minister. When we are in fellowship with one another, we take on these titles as well. Sometimes we are the fellow soldier, who sits with someone who is grieving, holding their hand and crying with them. Sometimes we are the one to gently remind the group that a particular discussion is starting to go in a direction that is not conducive to our beliefs. This is what fellowship looks like. We are one body with many parts. Each of us are crucial to the whole.

Reflections

Service

Isaiah 42:6b
"...And I will appoint You as a covenant to the people,
as a light to the nations."

Week Thirty-Seven   **Day Seven**

God is our example here as a "covenant to the people and light to the nations". What does it mean to be a light to the nations? I believe that this is accomplished, in part, in service work. My husband and I established and ran a home for girls who couldn't seem to stay off drugs and out of jail. Grace House was a faith-based organization. However, we decided not to cram the Bible and religion down their throats. We figured they had gotten enough of that throughout their lives. We did start every morning with a devotional time and the women were expected to attend church on Sunday mornings with us.

We lived with the women, so our every move was watched by these oh-so-suspicious roomies! But, without an exception, each one of them eventually asked us, "Why in the world would you have nine felons leeching off you?" Ah!!!! Foot in the door. This was our opportunity to talk about how God put this crazy idea in our head during our *first* year of marriage!! It was our time to tell them about Jesus. And we did. It is truly amazing how God uses us in service to Him!

Reflections

Worship

Galatians 1:10
"For am I now seeking the favor of men, or God...
If I were still trying to please men,
I would not be a bond servant of Christ."

Week Thirty-Eight   **Day One**

So, how strong is peer pressure? Never really thought about it much until I did. Years ago, I was doing some self-inventory work as part of a twelve step program. I thought I was a stand-alone guy, not subject to the whims or taunts of others, able to make up my own mind or decisions. Maybe not so much, the inventory revealed.

I wanted to please folks in a worldly way. I wanted to belong in a worldly way. I wanted to use bad language to feel a part of the group. Drinking and running after the ladies were a part of that as well. All very destructive actions and had their consequences in my life.

When we talk about worship, we are saying that we put God before all else. The ideals and ways of man or the world are no longer our driving force. Paul tells us here that if we are doing those things then we are not bound to God. Paul wants us to know that the world is going to try to continue to draw us near. We need to know it is one way or the other. We cannot live in both worlds. Obviously easier said than done at times but we worship a forgiving God who allows us to return if we choose a less desired path at times.

Reflections

Bible Reading

Titus 1:8, 9
"Be hospitable, loving what is good, sensible, just, devout,
self-controlled, holding fast the faithful word, which is
in accordance with the teaching, that he may be able
both to exhort in sound doctrine and to refute those who
contradict."

Week Thirty-Eight   **Day Two**

We have all met folks that we did not care to hang around for long. No real issues you could explain, they just did not seem to have the qualities you regarded as necessary for your friendship. These folks just seem to have some character issues that rubbed you the wrong way for some reason. You are not attempting to be judgmental but you just would not choose to have them in your inner circle. There is a good possibility that we come across the same way to some folks as well.

God's word tells us that we need to attract folks to us with our character. We need to earn the right to tell others the Good News of the Gospel. Our walk with God needs to be obvious to those around us. The Apostle Paul instructs one of His students in this very subject. In Titus 1:8, 9, he tells Titus to be "hospitable, loving what is good, sensible, just, devout, self-controlled, holding fast the faithful word…" We are to work towards these lofty goals expected by God by staying in His Word. It is through His Word we find the requirements and the strength necessary to meet them.

Reflections

Prayer

Revelation 5:8
"When He had taken the book, the four living creatures and the twenty-four elders fell down before the lamb, having each a harp, and golden bowls full of incense, which are the prayers of the saints."

Week Thirty-Eight   **Day Three**

As God closes out human history there are lots of things that are going to happen. There will be signs, events that take place that reveal the stages of this operation. Most likely those here on earth now will be in heaven taking part in another way. We will not be on the earth experiencing the judgments and the tribulation period.

Today John gives us some wonderful insight on what happens to our prayers. Here he tells us they end up in front of God. John describes them as incense burning before God, a pleasant aroma for God to inhale.

I'm not trying to unpack the Book of Revelation. I do want you to see the destination of our prayers. God hears them, they are like a sweet aroma before Him. I know this passage is about the End Times, yet the truth about prayer is the same. God sees our prayers as pleasure and wants the communication to be constant.

All the bowls, plagues, seals of judgments that are written about in John's vision are confusing. We can know for sure our prayers are heard and they please God. That is good news and I want to continue practicing these spiritual disciplines so I can stay in the correct posture before God.

Reflections

Meditation

Exodus 5:2
"Pharaoh said, 'Who is the Lord that I should obey
His voice to let Israel go?'"

Week Thirty-Eight   **Day Four**

Have you ever heard something from someone you really did not care for that got you thinking? It seems like there are some folks that as soon as they start speaking you turn them off, start playing with your phone or daydreaming. Maybe it is just me.

Yet, somehow you are present enough that you hear something. Maybe not earth shattering but a word, phrase or concept that gets you thinking. You try to blow it off because of who it came from but it sticks with you and you begin to roll it over in your head. Yep, hate when that happens.

Moses and Aaron march into Pharaoh's office and demand he let the people of God go. This is right at the beginning of the Exodus drama so there is still more to come between these two parties.

Pharaoh, the ruler of Egypt and a superpower at that time makes a good point. Normally we just blow him off as evil and want him to get his due. Nevertheless, he asks a real good question, "Who is this Lord I should obey?"

As a Pastor I have been asked that question a lot. I meditate often on that question because I know I need to know the answer - not just the words to say but feel the real call to faithfulness and obedience. Those who ask the question will know if you believe the answer or not.

Reflections

Physical Wellness

Joshua 4:24
"All the peoples of the earth may know that the hand of the
Lord is mighty, so that you may fear the Lord your God
forever."

Week Thirty-Eight   **Day Five**

When I first started playing little league baseball, we actually
had try-outs. The coaches would watch you hit, run, field and
throw to determine if they wanted to pick you. Rough, right?
Now everyone got put on a team but there was a position in
mind for you on the team when you were selected. Obviously
that little bit of exposure at the try outs could not tell the coach
very much but an initial impression was made.

Here the people of God were coming out of the desert and
had crossed the Jordon River on their way to take over Jericho.
They were instructed to leave a pile of stones in the river so
people could be reminded of God's power and might. Not just
the enemy but God's people as well needed to remember His
power and might.

We need to stay physically well for that same reason. Folks
look at us as Christians and should see something different
than they see in themselves. We are serious about being
prepared to do God's will. We must be a reminder of His
power and might, through our body, mind and spirit. The lost
need to know we are ready to help them along their spiritual
journey. Physical wellness is something tangible they can see
about our readiness.

Reflections

Fellowship

John 4:28, 29
"So, the woman left her water pot, and went into the city, and said to the men, come see a man who told me all things that I have done…"

I was told once that you can tell who your friends are if they were delighted to hear your good news. There are always plenty of folks that want to hear all the negative. They seem to thrive on just being grumpy and have a need to seek the worst in life to complain about. So, a true friend is rare and a blessing.

If you had a good day, had a cure for an illness or your kid did something great in school, who would you tell? Where could you go with this good news? The fellowship of believers, I hope. It is there we share what God has done for us and how He has blessed us. It is there where they are happy to hear about your successes and not jealous about them or resentful.

This lady Jesus has encountered had just heard some great news. Puzzling and strange to hear right off the bat, it encouraged her and gave her hope so she ran to share it with her community. Now, she was kind of an outcast but that did not stop her from wanting to share what she had learned with others.

To her credit she did not let her social standing get in her way. She wanted everyone to be as excited and full of hope as she was. Do we fellowship in that way? Do we want others to feel as blessed as we are? Are we wanting others to get the message of the Good News of Jesus? I hope so!

Reflections

Service

2 Samuel 9:3
"Is there not yet anyone of the house of Saul to whom I may
show the kindness of God?"

Week Thirty-Eight   **Day Seven**

Our Sunday school class has just finished up a study of King David. What a great guy and so human. The Bible relates his ups and downs and still he is labeled a man after God's own heart. I have always liked him but now I like him more, baggage and all.

Today we find him modeling a great way to serve others. He wants to help out one of his enemy's relatives. He and King Saul had a rocky history and it would seem normal for David not to want to have anything to do with his extended family. David sees it differently.

David was friends with Jonathan, King Saul's son. He did make a promise to look after his family when he became king. So that is part of the motivation for seeking this service opportunity. The bigger picture is that King David wanted to share his blessing with those around him. Sure, he made a promise but no one was alive to hold him to that.

We need to think the same way. We need to be proactive in our service discipline. Sure, sometime the opportunities just appear but more often than not there are plenty if we look for them.

Reflections

Worship

Galatians 2:16
"Nevertheless, knowing that man is not justified by the works of law, but through faith in Christ Jesus, even we have believed in Christ Jesus, so that we may be justified by faith in Christ and not by the works of the Law; since by the works of the Law no flesh will be justified."

Week Thirty-Nine   **Day One**

"Justified by faith...and not by works". Hmmm, so does this mean that I don't have to do service work? Uh, no. Faith in Christ means that we "know that we know that we know" God sent His only Son to die for our sins so that we may live forever in heaven with Him. A by-product of faith is service...and fellowship and prayer and worship and all the other spiritual disciplines.

By worshipping God, we intrinsically show our faith. And when we have faith in Christ, we can't help but worship Him. God knows if we believe or not. He knows our hearts (which is both sobering and comforting). The flip side is, when we truly believe our Father, we can't help but bust at the seams to worship Him, to praise Him, to simply be with Him. And what a wonderful place to be!

Reflections

Bible Reading

Philemon 1:20
"Yes, brother, let me benefit from you in the Lord, refresh
my heart in Christ."

Week Thirty-Nine   **Day Two**

Those of us who have children would gladly give them anything they needed to be successful. We might not spoil them or enable their addictions but we would certainly assist in any way we could. There are those also who serve those around them and sacrifice themselves for others. Most folks however will not take on other people's debts or vouch for them in personal affairs. We basically have enough to do to take care of our own issues. We have very little left over for anyone else, much less strangers. We justify our actions in many ways, usually by believing we ourselves are too limited in our own resources to be of much help.

The truth of the matter is God allowed His Son to die for us and Jesus went willingly to the cross for our sins. The biblical example they set hardly leaves any room for holding back on our part. The Apostle Paul gives this same advice to Philemon about his runaway slave Onesimus. In Philemon 1:20, Paul says to Philemon, "Brother let me benefit from you in the Lord; refresh my heart in Christ." Paul was asking Philemon to forgive Onesimus for running away, accept him back as a brother in Christ and to allow him to return to help Paul. God's Word asks us to look for ways to show His love in a practical way to those around us.

Reflections

Prayer

Luke 19:46a
"It is written, 'And My house shall be a house of prayer...'"

There were actually two occasions where Jesus cleansed the temple. The first was right after He turned water into wine during a Jewish wedding in Cana. The second occurred as Jesus was returning to Jerusalem for the Passover (on what became Palm Sunday). This is Luke's account of the infamous "cleansing of the temple". Man, He wasn't kidding when He told the merchants and tax collectors that His church was a house of prayer! He knocked stuff over and basically tore down the merchant area.

Just as the church is part of the body, so am I. And I hope "my house" is one of prayer. As I have confided before, there are times where my "house" is full of stuff that shouldn't be there. That's when I have to let the Holy Spirit in to knock stuff over and tear down my "merchant area" and return God's temple (my body) to one of prayer.

Reflections

Meditation

Leviticus 10:10
"And so to make a distinction between the Holy and the
profane..."

Week Thirty-Nine   **Day Four**

I'm a gardener. I love everything about it–planning, planting, dead-heading, weeding, harvesting–the whole shebang. But the best thing, for me, about gardening is being with Jesus. I don't know how long I've been aware of His presence when I'm in the garden, but it's now what draws me to the dirt. Gardening with Jesus. It is the sweetest time. I talk, He listens. He talks, I listen. It truly is as if He were physically there with me! This is meditation; and for me, at its finest.

Meditation is an intimate time between you and God. It can be done anytime, anywhere. If you are new to it, hang in there. It, like most things, takes time and "practice". I'm sure when I was first aware of Jesus in the garden with me, I squandered a lot of that time letting my mind wander off and ignoring what He had to say. Not to say that still doesn't happen from time to time, but for the most part I am fully aware of His presence and love, support and guidance.

Find a spot or time where you can completely pay attention. For me, sitting in a quiet room, in a position that will render my body useless for a time, doesn't work. It may for you... just like gardening might not be your cup of tea. The point is, start. And make it a daily part of your life. The payoff is phenomenal!

Reflections

Physical Wellness

Ruth 2:2
"Please let me go to the fields and glean among the ears of grain..."

Week Thirty-Nine   **Day Five**

A couple of weeks ago, I wrote about physical wellness and addictions, self-harm, and other things we do to ourselves that are physically harmful. As I sit to write today, I think about folks with serious physical maladies and afflictions they were born with or developed later in life – sufferings not generated by them, but simply handed to them. How does the spiritual discipline of physical wellness work for these amazing people?

In his second letter to the Corinthians, Paul discloses that he had been given "a thorn in the flesh" which he contends was a "messenger of Satan" (2 Cor. 12:7). It drives me nuts that no details of this thorn is ever revealed, but that's because I'm nosy. It turns out, the ambiguity of this thorn enables all of us to empathize and not discard Paul's experience if we don't have the same affliction. The existence of a physical unwellness does not mean a believer has sinned or lacks faith. In fact, God Himself tells us that, "My grace is sufficient for you, for My power is made perfect in weakness" (2 Cor. 12:9). I'm sure this can be a hard pill to swallow for those suffering, but please know that God has big things planned for you!

Reflections

Fellowship

John 10:16
"I have other sheep, which are not of this fold; I must bring them also, and they will hear My voice; and they will become one flock with one shepherd."

Week Thirty-Nine   **Day Six**

So much of my time writing this devotion was done smack-dab in the middle of the 2020 COVID-19 pandemic, a time of social distancing and purposefully staying away from others. We are seeing a sharp decline in church attendance (as most of the churches can only have 50% of their congregation gathered at any one time). And for those that are having drive-in services or honoring the social distancing in the physical churches, how much fellowship is happening? What does fellowship look like now?

Many are turning toward social media and tools like Google Hangout and Zoom to meet. Some are making sure those that have chosen to stay at home are getting their groceries, medications, etc. But, folks, we can still fellowship from 6 feet away. Form a group that meets in the park once a week (or online, if that serves better). Make sure that you are connecting with those people in your life who love you (and God) and will hold you accountable. Somehow, some way make sure you are spending time with other Christians—and do it safely!

Reflections

Service

Exodus 2:3
"But when she could hide him no longer, she got him a wicker basket and covered it over with tar and pitch. Then she put the child into it and set it among the reeds by the bank of the Nile."

Week Thirty-Nine   **Day Seven**

Well, after yesterday's writing about social distancing and fellowship, today's spiritual discipline of service is a terrific follow-up. I mentioned that I'm writing during the COVID-19 pandemic. A time of social distancing – deliberately not being in physical contact with other people – gives us all a chance to up our service game. We all know people who have to be extra careful during this time as they are in the group who may not fair well if infected. Reach out to these precious people. Run errands. Mow yards. Sit on their front porch (with masks and 6 feet between you) and listen. Remember, so many of these people are desperately lonely...and probably scared. Just be with them.

My mom has been writing a newsy letter to her Sunday School women on a regular basis. She lets them know what's going on in her world, but also lets them know they aren't alone and that someone is thinking about them. A younger friend of mine calls her "stay-at-home peeps" weekly. She prays, quotes Scripture, and reminds her friends that God knows what He is doing. This is service. So, this week, I challenge you to reach out to someone you know is self-isolating because of the pandemic. And then do it the next week....and the one after that!

Reflections

Worship

Proverbs 1:7
"The fear of the Lord is the beginning of knowledge; fools despise wisdom and instruction."

Week Forty   **Day One**

The motto of the wisdom teachers and the theme of the Book of Proverbs is that the fear of the Lord is the starting point and essence of wisdom. Fear is a reverence for God expressed in submission to His will. Wisdom is not acquired by a mechanical formula but through a right relationship with God.

Today the old fire and brimstone preaching of the past is hard to fathom. Why cause guilt and cause fear from the pulpit? God is not someone to fear! He is love and compassion and forgiveness.

I loved my Dad but a lot of the reason I was obedient was fear of the sound of that belt being pulled through his belt loops. He loved me fiercely so he disciplined me. I was not afraid of my Dad; I had a healthy respect for his leadership technique.

We worship God with an awe and reverence because of who He is. Consequently, He says that is the beginning of wisdom. There is a correlation we should keep in mind as we develop our worship discipline. Understand, God will punish and will hold us accountable. He disciplines those He loves.

Reflections

Bible Reading

Hebrews 2:1
"For this reason, we pay much closer attention to what we
have heard, lest we drift away from it."

Week Forty   **Day Two**

When I was growing up, when summer vacation came around
my parents made us kids do schoolwork most weekday
mornings. They did not want us to go through "summer brain
dump," so in the fall we could start off our new school year
in good shape. Of course, I always thought it was cruel and
unusual punishment but each fall, when school started again,
I was glad I had exercised my brain during the summer. It is
easy to forget the things we have learned unless we continue
to refresh our memories. The things we do not use often we
lose proficiency with.

The author of the Book of Hebrews wants to make sure
his readers realize they need to stay abreast of the principles
of this "new way," Christianity. In Hebrews 2:1, the author
writes, "we must pay much closer attention to what we have
heard, lest we drift away from it." God's Word is important in
so many ways. We could study for the rest of our lives and still
really only scratch the surface. It is our responsibility to stay
current in God's Word and to use it to grow spiritually. As we
grow, we move deeper and deeper into the Bible for revelation
from God.

Reflections

Prayer

Psalms 145:18
"The Lord is near to all who call upon Him, to all who call upon Him in truth."

Week Forty   **Day Three**

We pray to God because we believe He is the Author, Creator and Sustainer of the universe. We pray to Him because we believe He loves us and wants the best for us. We pray to God because He says He hears our prayers. Mostly we pray to God because we believe He is truth.

I cannot unpack all the character traits of God. There is no way to I have enough room. I will say His primary character is that He is truth. He only operates in that realm. He knows only how to give out truth and will only accept truth from us. He knows the difference in truth and what we try to feed Him sometimes.

We often wonder why our prayer life seems unproductive. We cannot understand why our prayers seem to go unanswered. We get frustrated with our communication times with God, is He listening?

God deals in truth. He does not listen to anything but truth. We cannot approach Him with anything less and expect a flow of communication to begin. James says, "we ask and do not receive because we ask wrongly..." (James 4:3) There is a way to be correct before God and the truth is it. He knows the truth already; He wants us to be honest enough to recognize it as well.

Reflections

Meditation

Romans 12:2
"Do not be conformed to this world, but be transformed by the renewing of your mind, that you may prove what the will of God is."

Week Forty   **Day Four**

If you ever attend any twelve step meeting there is a phrase you will hear often, "Our best thinking got us here!" Meaning, the way we made decisions and the process we used to run our life led us to this point. Our addiction is a direct result of our faulty decision making process. If we were so smart how did we end up in a twelve step program?

If we want to recover from our addiction there has to be a change. We have to begin to view certain things in a different light. We have to admit we have a problem then apply the help that is offered from those who have successfully moved forward, clean and sober. When it comes to our addiction our thinking, mental process or behavioral traits need an overhaul, a renewing.

Paul is saying the same thing to the folks in Rome. Your old way of viewing God and your need to participate in His plan is off. Begin to think like Him. Allow the Holy Spirit to lead you into the correct posture before Him.

We must begin to listen during our times of meditation. God will help us renew our mind. He will help us transform our mental process to match up with His. Seeing things His way is refreshing and a lot easier than our way.

Reflections

Physical Wellness

1 Samuel 1:5
"To Hannah he would give a double portion…but the Lord closed her womb."

Week Forty   **Day Five**

There are times as we seek to stay physical well, we just cannot meet our goals. No matter what we do, we do not seem to be able to add to our bench press, decrease our two mile time or the scale just seems to keep lying about our weight. Even with a disciplined routine we seem to be stalemated, not moving anywhere. It is frustrating and concerning. We just wonder, "What in the world is the issue?"

Samuel's mom, Hannah, was thinking the same thing. She was spiritually fit, doing everything she could to stay on track. Yet, still no conception would happen. Her husband would even give her double portions for the temple sacrifice so she could feel proactive in working on her condition. Still she could not conceive.

Our job is to do the best we can. We know what to do that is healthy and beneficial to our cause of physical wellness. We stay on target, aware of the frustrations and keep doing the next correct thing. God is in charge of the outcome. He knows we are working hard and will bless that effort. He will give us the increase in His time. Our job is to stay faithful to the goal and continually seek to stay fit. Keep up the good work, God sees it!

Reflections

Fellowship

1 Kings 17:9
"Arise, go to Zarephath...
I have commanded a widow there to provide for you."

Week Forty   **Day Six**

Have you ever been traveling and gotten lonely? You are somewhere outside your normal stomping grounds and do not know anyone. You long for your normal fellowship and the comforts of those surroundings. I sure felt that way in prison. I was in a strange, hostile environment wondering how I would make it without the fellowship of folks I had come to depend on. Weird and scary.

Elijah is being sent away from his homeland because of the severe drought that was consuming it. God told him to go outside this area and that He would take care of him. God wanted Elijah to be away from the enemies who were looking for him. God knew he was being blamed for the current drought conditions.

God provided fellowship for him. A lady and her son were obedient to God and provided for him. God gave him a place where he could find fellowship. He could be cared for and he could care for them as well.

God did the same thing for me in prison. I was able to participate in some small group Bible studies and a weekly twelve step group. He led me to brothers in Christ that I was able to fellowship with safely. There is no way I could have dealt with that environment without the fellowship God saw fit to lead me to.

Reflections

Service

Mathew 25:40
"Truly I say to you, to the extent that you did it to one of these brothers of Mine, even the least of them, you did it to Me."

Week Forty   **Day Seven**

Very often we are asked to serve outside our comfort zone. It is easy to serve those in our families, Sunday school or civic groups. It's not so easy to step out and serve those we are less familiar with. It's even harder when we deem them less than us. I wrote a book called "Labels". Read it, it will help you with this last group.

Matthew was a tax collector. He knew what it was like to be despised and be considered "less than." It is fitting that he was led to emphasize this part of one of Jesus' discourses. He did not necessarily need to be served in a worldly view. He had money and a station in life. God still chose Him so he could learn to serve.

Jesus makes service such a big deal that He relates service to those we deem less than as service to Him. Every time we serve another, we serve God. We not only do His work on this earth. We feed Him. We keep Him from being thirsty. We make sure He is clothed. That changes things, right?

Reflections

Worship

Ecclesiastes 3:14a
"I know that everything God does will remain forever..."

Week Forty-One   **Day One**

When we know – I mean really know, like how we know the sun is going to rise tomorrow – that everything God does "will remain forever", we are then truly worshipping God. Worship is our way of showing and observing our deep reverence towards God. It is a show of acknowledgement that the Lord God Almighty exists. It is our time to thank God and praise God and lift Him up to the place He belongs.

Charlie tells us that "worship is a must to know the heart and mind of God" (When Life Shows Up, pg. 89). He goes on to say that worship allows us to get in the "right posture" in order to deepen our understanding, our faith, and our obedience. For those of us who are thirsty for Him, the practice of worshipping God becomes second nature as our relationship and understanding of God intensifies.

Reflections

Bible Reading

Hebrews 6:1
"Therefore leaving the elementary teachings about Christ, let us press on to maturity...."

Week Forty-One   **Day Two**

In life, unless you are steadily moving forward, you will get run over. This movement does not have to be swift or even monumental, but there always needs to be movement. We humans do not have the luxury to stay in one place physically, mentally or spiritually. Complacency and inactivity allow the forces of the world to slowly pick away at our defenses and begin to make inroads on our development. If we are standing still, we are a sure target for the evil one to attempt to claim us for his own.

The author of the Book of Hebrews understood this concept. In Hebrews 6:1, he tells his readers they should, "...leave the elementary teaching about Christ, let us move forward on to maturity..." We should always be moving forward toward the goals God has for us. God's Word lets us know these goals, helps us understand the "how's" we need to accomplish this movement. We are not alone in this, we need just to start and God, through His Word, will reveal the next step to us.

Reflections

Prayer

2 Chronicles 7:14
"My people who are called by My name humble themselves
and pray and seek My face and turn from their wicked ways,
then I will hear from heaven, will forgive their sins and will
heal their land."

Week Forty-One   **Day Three**

Thankfully, we have a "users' manual" (aka—the Bible) to tell us how to do everything. In this case, we are told to pray for our country and our leaders. Over and over, Scripture tells us what God expects from us and how to do it. And He does hear us and will respond. Here, we are reminded that before we come to God in prayer, we must first humble ourselves, seek His face, and turn from our evil ways. Before we come to God, we must confess our sins and humbly ask Him to forgive us. It is only then that we can see God's face. And as I write this in the midst of the COVID-19 lockdown, our nation, our world, and those in authority need our prayers more than ever!

Reflections

Meditation

1 Corinthians 10:23a
"All things are lawful, but not all things are profitable."

Week Forty-One   **Day Four**

Paul, in his first letter to the Corinthians, is actually talking about the question of eating meat that had been offered to idols. The point he is making is that on the surface oftentimes our actions are *legal* but looking at them in a deeper way can cause the individual, the church as a whole, and others harm. Throughout the ages, this has been a stumbling block for Christians: misunderstanding what it means to be free in Christ. the liberty of free-will, and the restrictive rules of legalism.

Just because our sins are forgiven does not give us carte blanche to do whatever we want. Many things that are not sinful in and of themselves could certainly be a problem for another person. As we meditate on our actions and decisions, we must be aware of this free-will and how it impacts us as followers of Christ, but always how it is received by others. We are warned, time and time again, about not being stumbling blocks to other Christians as well as non-believers. So, as we meditate, we need to make sure that our actions—albeit seemingly okay—don't cause another to falter in his/her belief. Ask yourself: Will God be pleased by this decision? Is this helping or hindering another? Does this build me and others up? God'll let you know. Just ask Him.

Reflections

Physical Wellness

2 Samuel 9:3b
"There is still a son of Jonathan
who is crippled in both feet…"

Week Forty-One   **Day Five**

It seems I've been on a "physical imperfections" kick the last couple of weeks. In the context of physical wellness as a spiritual discipline, physical maladies and un-wellness must be addressed. I often joke that when God put me together, He used spare parts from other people: my spine is crooked; one leg is shorter than the other; one of my heart valves leaks. The Bible is full of folks who are blind and crippled. Many of us have diseases and conditions that rendered our body not so perfect.

The spiritual discipline of physical wellness is not about the body you were handed or the body that has deteriorated from outside sources. It is about honoring our bodies—as is. It is about acknowledging the physical vessel our souls and minds inhabit. It is about thanking God for what He has provided and treating our physical selves as the holy temple of our Maker.

Reflections

Fellowship

Acts 8:26
"But an angel of the Lord spoke to Philip saying,
'Get up and go south'..."

Week Forty-One   **Day Six**

So, the angel tells Philip to "go south" and by doing so, he runs into an Ethiopian eunuch. Turns out, the eunuch was reading the prophet Isaiah and admitted that he didn't quite understand what he was reading. Philip explains the text to the eunuch and as a result, the eunuch accepts Christ and Philip baptizes him.

Fellowship is something we do with no barriers or conditions; we shouldn't care if someone is old or young, their race or ethnic origin should not matter to us, and a person's physical condition should not preclude them from the Good News. Any time we are in the presence of others, we are faced with the opportunity of fellowship. How many times have you missed opportunities? In the next week, be more aware of occasions in which God has placed you to practice this spiritual discipline.

Reflections

Service

Psalms 15:2
"He who walks with integrity, and works with righteousness,
and speaks the truth in his heart."

Week Forty-One   **Day Seven**

By now we know that service work is mandatory for us Christians. We have been tasked with doing it. But it doesn't end there. This verse tells us that our very beings must walk the walk, talk the talk. As we are engaged in our daily lives, we must do so with integrity, righteousness, and truth. How many times have you been jammed up because a Christian's words and actions don't sync up? How many time have we jammed up someone else because of the same thing?

So, whether we are in the midst of helping others or just at the grocery store getting supplies, we must conduct ourselves in a manner that will bring others to Christ. This *is* the ultimate service work! If we are known for lying and manipulating and using others, for example, who would want to be part of that? We must always be aware that others are watching and we simply have to live our lives based on the way Jesus did.

Reflections

Worship

The Song of Solomon 2:1
"I am the Rose of Sharon, the lily of the valley."

Week Forty-Two   **Day One**

This book presents a vivid picture of faithful love and deepening communion. The intimate terms used only illustrate the wonderful love between Christ and the Christian. From the earliest days the Jews saw in this story a picture of the relationship between God and Israel. This relationship is also used to describe the bond between Christ and the church. The universal church, all believers and our local churches.

Solomon is pointing out that God is beauty, perfection and something that enhances our life. There is lots of imagery in this book but it all points to reasons we need to be in faithful worship with God.

My life is better with God in it. My life run on my own was not as peaceful and efficient as when He is running it. I worship God because I was lost and now have direction. I was in chaos and now I am in peace. I was a mess and He has made me a message.

God sees us for who we are and has a plan to move us closer to Him. We worship Him because we believe He can and will make our life better. Mostly we worship because He secured our place in heaven with the death of His Son.

Reflections

Bible Reading

James 1:16, 17
"Do not be deceived my beloved brethren. Every good thing bestowed and every perfect gift is from above, coming down from the Father of lights, with whom there is no variation, or shifting shadow."

Week Forty-Two   **Day Two**

There are lots of folks in the world who do not have our best interests at heart. That of course is no big surprise but maybe they are closer to you than you think. Face it, we humans are spring loaded to selfish and self-centered actions. The best of us fall into this trap, while others take it to a new level of art form. The question is what do we do about it?

James, the brother of Jesus in his book gives a good answer. In James 1:16, 17 he tells his readers to "not be deceived…" James was speaking about temptation but the advice is good in all areas of our life. He goes on to say that "every good thing, bestowed and every perfect gift is from above, coming from the Father…" Unless we know it is from God, we do not need it, no matter how much we try to convince ourselves. God's Word helps us determine from where our needs are met and what is just plain temptation or wants.

Reflections

Prayer

Isaiah 7:11
"Ask a sign for yourself from the Lord your God; make it
deep as Sheol or high as heaven."

Week Forty-Two   **Day Three**

Remember back in school when you were being taught
something by your teacher and you just could not get it. Even
when the other kids around you seemed to get it you could not.
You could grasp a lot of things you were learning but this one
concept seemed to evade you.

Teachers want you to learn this stuff. They are not trying
to hold back so certain students would be frustrated and feel
less than by the other kids. In fact, usually there was time for
extra tutoring or extra assignments so you could work a little
more to help turn the light bulb on.

Here Isaiah is trying to do just that. He is trying to help
Ahaz to understand his thinking is going to get him in trouble,
with God and the folks he thinks he can depend on. Isaiah says
ask for a sign or something, God will prove what I am telling
you is the truth.

Prayer helps us get what God is saying. He wants us to
understand and knows we often do not. Prayer puts us before
Him so we can get extra tutoring if we need it. We know
very little, as it turns out, compared to God. Yet, He will
patiently give us extra assignments so we can get that light
bulb turned on.

Reflections

Meditation

Galatians 2:20
"I have been crucified with Christ; and it is no longer I who live but Christ lives in me; and the life I live in the flesh I live by faith in the Son of God, who loved me and delivered Himself up for me."

Week Forty-Two   **Day Four**

Crucifixion with Christ means death to or separation from the reigning power of the old sinful life and freedom to experience the power of the resurrection life of Christ by faith. If we are to belong to God we must stop belonging to the world. There is no way God will have us if we are the world's.

Well that seems like deep theology, I know. It is deep and it is the basis of our belief as Christians. We are no longer to live in our old sinful patterns. We have been forgiven and cleansed so we can be useful to God. We take on faith that this rejuvenation will put us in the Lamb's Book of Life and our future is secured.

Lots to think about. Paul wants us to know that he is filled with God and is now allowing Him to lead, guide and direct him. This direction is sometimes hard to determine. It gets easier as we practice meditation. We allow God to speak to us and the Holy Spirit to interpret for us so we can apply His Words, direction to our life. Take time to practice hearing from God. Total submersion in His will is the easiest way to hear more clearly.

Reflections

Physical Wellness

1 Kings 4:29
"Now God gave Solomon wisdom and very great discernment and breath of mind like the sand that is on the seashore."

Week Forty-Two   **Day Five**

All we have comes from God. There is nothing on this earth that was not made by God. Men can create, form, build and assemble but it is God who made the raw materials. All our abilities come from God. We in ourselves can do nothing. We are not smart enough, gifted or talented or capable enough to accomplish anything on our own. These are just the facts.

Kind of a jab in the gut for me. I never thought I was all that but I did think I was something. Apparently, I was not; sadly, I was the last one to know. Those around knew my limitations but I could not see them.

The author of Kings tells us that God gave Solomon all that was necessary for him to be the wisest and richest king ever. You can track some of these folks God has gifted and you see what happens when they begin to think they did it all on their own.

Our job is to be in constant preparation. God will provide the opportunities for our success. We stay physically ready to meet the challenges God gives us. We want to be ready for anything He sees fit to assign us to. If we feel we are being underutilized maybe it is because we are not correctly utilizing what God has given us.

Reflections

Fellowship

Colossians 3:14
"And beyond all these things put on love, which is the
perfect bond of unity."

Week Forty-Two   **Day Six**

There is nothing like the feeling of being loved. There is a warmth and a bond that appears when we are loved. There is a feeling of security when we are loved. Mostly there is peace and contentment in our lives that comes from being loved.

John, in his gospel says, "By this all men will know that you are My disciples, if you have love for one another" (John 13:35). Love looks so different from what happens in the world that folks will immediately recognize that you come from some other direction.

Paul wants us to understand that love is the crowning Christian characteristic. After he lists a few other character traits we Christians should be displaying, love is the most important. Why is it important? Paul says because it symbolizes our unity. Our fellowship is recognized for its love. John said the same thing: they will know us by our love.

We need to stand out as different from what the world offers as answers. We have the answer: faith in God. We will not be seen as having any answer if we are repulsive and exclude folks. We are commanded to love all throughout God's Word. It has always been the key to our spiritual growth and Christian journey. Fellowship is where we practice giving and receiving love. Then we can take it out to a lost and dying world.

Reflections

Service

Proverbs 10:5
"He who gathers in summer is a son who acts wisely, but he who sleeps in harvest is a son who acts shameful."

Week Forty-Two   **Day Seven**

A wise son is one who fears and obeys God and makes a successful application of knowledge in everyday dealings. The foolish one is insensible and insensitive to oral truth, acting without regard to it and to his own destruction. Makes sense to me.

If we want to be the "wise son," we need to not be selfish and self-centered. The root of all our problems generally comes from those traits. Society will say that we must take care of "number one." God says that we must be willing to do things for others so we can receive His blessings.

Solomon is telling us that the wise son is going to do what is necessary despite what he feels like or even against his own desires. The wise person will go ahead and get up to serve or work or do the next right thing. It sounds easy but so often we get tangled up in our own self that we cannot see how debilitating our actions are.

When we serve, we get out of our own head. We begin to get clarity about what is truly important. We get on track to be that "wise son," looking to move forward in our spiritual journey by keeping in focus the mundane duties of life.

Reflections

Worship

Ruth 4:14
"...Blessed is the Lord who has not left you without a
redeemer today..."

Week Forty-Three   **Day One**

Naomi lost her husband and two sons and was left with only two daughters-in-law, Ruth and Orpah. So, Naomi decides to return to her native Bethlehem and encourages her daughters-in-law to return to their families. Orpah decides to go back to her people, but Ruth goes with Naomi. After relocating to Bethlehem, Ruth meets a local man, Boaz, gets married, and has a son. This son is in the lineage of Jesus (a descendent of David). So now, not only does Naomi have a male relative (Boaz) to take care of her, she now has a grandson.

We must remember that God's plan for our lives is perfect. Even when we can't figure out what God's plan is, He knows it. And it's always for good (Romans 8:28). During our worship time, let's remember this and acknowledge to God that we trust His loving judgement and plan.

Reflections

Bible Reading

James 4:17
"Therefore, to one who knows the right thing to do and does
not do it, to him it is sin."

Week Forty-Three   **Day Two**

If you are able to read and work through this devotional then
you have enough going for you to know what sin is. The
world tries to make wrong and right this mass of gray so it
is impossible to know the difference. They do this because it
creates for them a doubt about if something is actually right or
wrong. This lessens the guilt and frees the conscience. Masking
sin does not take away the judgment that ultimately will be
exacted for all sinful actions.

James, the preacher of the church in Jerusalem and the
brother of Jesus, gives us some sage clarification on this point.
In James 4:17, he says, "Therefore to one who knows the right
thing to do, and does not do it, to him it is sin." We who call
ourselves Christians are going to be held to a greater standard
than the lost around us. We cannot create these gray areas
like the world around us. God's Word is clear, eliminates the
gray and provides a very negotiable path to the truth. We just
need to seek it.

Reflections

Prayer

Zachariah 10:1
"Ask rain from the Lord...
and He will give them showers of rain..."

Week Forty-Three   **Day Three**

Do you ever pray for something and get more than you had ever dreamed (or even prayed for)? That's our God. He's big. And gracious. And kind. And sometimes a show-off! I say this somewhat tongue-in-cheek, but really, haven't you seen Him do something amazing when average would have sufficed? And let's not downplay the "insignificant" stuff we pray for – the light staying green just long enough to get through; or a snow day when we're late on an assignment. He listens. He really hears us. And He doesn't just let us get through the light, He lets five more cars go! And that snow day? He gives us a big ol' storm, giving us days to get the assignment plus everything else done! Truly amazing.

Prayer is an intimate time between you and God. He wants to hear from us. He wants to know everything about us. He seizes each word we utter. Let's not leave Him hanging.

Reflections

Meditation

Ephesians 6:11
"Put on the full armor of God, so that you will be able to
stand firm against the schemes of the devil."

Week Forty-Three   **Day Four**

I can get all caught up in the "What if" game. I can spend some considerable time playing out all the different outcomes in a situation and plan some elaborate comebacks that make me look brilliant. However, I don't spend nearly that much time and energy planning my spiritual warfare. Paul discusses this very thing in Ephesians (6:10 – 20). He goes into great detail about the tools given us to fight a successful battle against evil. And the fact that he uses the different components of real battle armor indicates that we have to be thoughtful and intentional about using these tools.

That's why these seven spiritual disciplines are so important. They *are* our armor. Just like a Roman soldier would not live very long in battle without his armor, so we, too, won't make it very long without ours.

Reflections

Physical Wellness

Ecclesiastes 3:11
"There is an appointed time for everything, and there is a
time for every event under heaven."

Week Forty-Three   **Day Five**

Pete Seeger put the words of Solomon in a song, "Turn! Turn!
Turn! (To Everything There is a Season)" in the late 1950's. It
was then recorded and released by The Byrds and climbed to
number one on the Billboard Hot 200 chart on December 4,
1965. King Solomon penned his words nearly a gazillion years
ago and they were true in the 1960s and they are true today.

We are on this earth for a reason – for a specific purpose –
and for a season. God made us with a body, a mind, and a spirit
with a complexity and significance to our very being. Solomon
wants us to know that we worship a God who wants us to be
healthy in all facets of our life and reminds us that this same
God intentionally put us here to fulfill His plan. There is a
beginning and an end to our life: what are we doing with the
in-between? Are we honoring God's purpose for us? Are we
carrying out His plan? As Solomon's words reminds us, there
is a time and season for everything.

Reflections

Fellowship

Hebrews 3:12
"Take care, brethren, that there not be in any one of you an evil, unbelieving heart that falls away from the living God."

Week Forty-Three   **Day Six**

There's a lot of talk in the Bible about how the Church is made up of many members, each with its own purpose, all very necessary. What happens when one part quits playing nicely with others? Think about when Israel lost faith in God. Those people wandered around in the desert for forty years! That generation was denied access to the Promise Land because, as a collective people, they turned from God. That's what happens.

As we fellowship with one another we lift one another up, sharing burdens, rejoicing together. We also have to be vigilant about the evil, unbelieving heart that sometimes comes upon us. We must be cognizant of the damage that can be done – and the consequences that ensue – when we, as a collective group, let one person invest the faith we have in God. (And as a side note, of course, we are given instructions on how to handle this type of situation. See Matthew 18:15-17.)

Reflections

Service

Genesis 29:20
"So Jacob served seven years for Rachel and they seemed to
him but a few days."

Week Forty-Three   **Day Seven**

Okay, some background: so, Jacob goes on a journey, in which he bumps into a relative, Laban, and meets his daughter, Rachel. Jacob falls in love with her and strikes a deal with Laban: Jacob will work for Laban for seven years in return for Rachel as his wife. Laban ends up reneging on the deal, marrying his eldest daughter to Jacob instead and requiring another seven years of work for Rachel. Jacob does it! He works, for free, for his father-in-law, who has already screwed him, so that he can marry Rachel! That's some dedication.

What, in your life, is so important to you that you'd work for free for fourteen – or even seven – years of your life? Seems like a crazy question, but once you get to thinking about it, I bet we all could actually come up with some ideas. You see, when we are motivated by something we desire, we will do almost anything, pay almost any price. That's the way it is when you're "working for the Lord". The insurmountable all of a sudden seems easy and doable. For those of us that love God and long to be with Him, sufferings of this world and present time are nothing.

Reflections

Worship

Esther 4:14
"For if you remain silent at this time, relief and deliverance
will arise for the Jews from another place and you and your
father's house will perish. And who knows whether you have
not attained royalty for such a time as this?"

Week Forty-Four   **Day One**

It is always nice when things just turn out right. The line you
get in at the store moves quickly. The gas pump actually works.
The elevator stays open long enough for you to get in on time.
The traffic lights seem to all be green when you are running a
little late. I could go on but you get the point, right?

Those things are nice because mostly they do not happen.
Life is good but rarely does it seem like everything is going
your way. Not that it is supposed to, but it seems like a balance
would be nice. Life is full of challenges and it is just enjoyable
when things just seem to line up.

God is in control and with His plan everything lines up.
Just because we do not see it or do not understand it does not
mean it is not just as He planned it. My way is always hit or
miss. God's way is always exactly right.

We worship God because like Mordecai, we know that
God has a plan. If we do not get on board, He will just get
someone else who is willing to be obedient to execute it for
Him. I am so glad I am not God and I am sure everyone who
knows me is glad as well.

Reflections

Bible Reading

1 Peter 1:13
"But to the degree that you share the sufferings of Christ,
keep on rejoicing; so that also at the revelation of His glory,
you may rejoice with exultation."

Week Forty-Four   **Day Two**

I remember as a kid my father taking me to look at the stars as part of a Cub Scout project. He said if I looked closely, I might see a falling star. For a fourth grader that seemed great. Sure enough after, what seemed hours, I actually saw a falling star. That was exciting and I felt like a miracle had happened. My dad said, "Yep it's a miracle but you saw it because you were looking!" Now years later I still look for falling stars and realize the only way to see them is by looking.

Life goes on all around us; we see but do not look. Evil lurks around us as well and we have the same problem, we see but do not look. Peter, the strong disciple of Jesus, spoke of how to handle this problem. In 1 Peter 1:13, he tells his readers to "gird up your minds for action, keep sober..." He is saying to be prepared for the good and bad. Look for a miracle as well as for the evil around you. Do not be surprised by either event. The Bible helps us stay focused, teaches us what to look for and from where we can receive help when we need it.

Reflections

Prayer

Mark 11:24
"Therefore, I say to you, all things for which you pray and ask, believe that you have received them, and they shall be granted to you."

Week Forty-Four   **Day Three**

One of the nice things about having a good relationship with my brother and sister is our ability to communicate. So, we have known each other all our lives and are pretty familiar with each other's character. We know each other's likes and dislikes. We know a lot about each other's abilities. We know each other's boundaries as well.

If I need help with something, or a sounding board or advice I know which one to ask. They both have different areas of expertise. More importantly I know what not to ask of each one as well. We are all willing to do whatever we can to help each other but we do all have limits.

Prayer helps us understand God's limits. Today we read that God is willing to help us in any way. There is no limit to what God can do. He is willing to bring all His ability in pursuit of our needs. He operates at a different level, has access to more knowledge and knows what is good or bad for us. If we ask and He knows it is not beneficial to His plan it will not happen. If it is beneficial to His plan, there is nothing that can stop it from happening.

Reflections

Meditation

Ecclesiastes 5:1
"Guard your steps as you go to the house of God and draw near to listen rather than to offer the sacrifice of fools; for they do not know they are doing evil."

Week Forty-Four **Day Four**

Have you ever heard someone say, "Measure twice and cut once?" Carpenters say it a lot but it is good advice for anyone making decisions. Take a good look at what you are about to do before you do it. It is a lot easier to move forward if you are not always correcting past mistakes. When possible, it is always better to double check before hitting the "send" button.

So often in our spiritual life we are haphazard about our approach. We are not intentional about our approach to our spiritual disciplines. We recklessly move through our meditation without considering our posture before God.

Solomon is talking here specifically about careless worship and sets forth some concerns for proper worship. He is exhorting his people to be careful, attentive, and listen with a view to obedience.

That is what our meditation time should be like. God wants us to meet with Him and share our life. He wants us to listen and grow. God is God and can only be approached a certain way. If not then we will be unsuccessful in our spiritual journey. He is not a stickler like the Jewish leaders of old but He is God and we need to approach Him with sincerity and reverence.

Reflections

Physical Wellness

Proverbs 19:20
"Listen to counsel and accept discipline, that you may be
wise the rest of your days."

Week Forty-Four   **Day Five**

Part of our spiritual journey is the ability to be taught. In our twelve step process we teach newly arrived folks fighting addiction that they need to get "teachable." Whatever they were doing obviously was not working because they are wrestling with unsuccessfully treated addictions.

No one likes being told what to do, that is the rub. If we were good direction takers, we would not be where we are at a lot of times in our life. I sure wish I had listened to a few people in my young adult life. I may have avoided a lot of heartache and pain my addiction caused me.

Physical wellness is no different. If we are to be prepared to do God's work we need to learn how to do so. There are folks further along in their spiritual journey than we are who are more than willing to help. Diet, exercise, medical needs and rest requirements are just a few things that aide in our physical development. All things we can learn and soon can become second nature. We need to listen to wise counsel and accept the discipline when needed. God wants the best for us and provides teachers as we need them. Another saying I like, "When the student is ready the teacher will appear."

Reflections

Fellowship

2 Timothy 4:5
"Be sober in all things, endure hardship, do the work of an evangelist, fulfill your ministry."

Week Forty-Four   **Day Six**

Timothy is Paul's protégé. Paul sends him out to different churches to teach and encourage folks. Both letters to Timothy are called the "Pastoral Epistles." They are intended to help guide Timothy in his dealing with these folks adapting to this young Christian faith.

The fellowship of believers was growing by leaps and bounds. Paul's ministry was extremely successful. God was bringing an increase that was phenomenal. This new "Way" was so different from what the believers had previously dealt with that the growing pains were abundant.

This message is not just for Timothy or the early church. It rings true for us today. As a fellowship we must be on point for our primary purpose. That purpose is to be the kind of believers that can stand up and share their faith. Our job as Christians, as a fellowship, is to be God's army determined to spread His Word to a lost and dying world.

Our strength comes from God through the fellowship. Our knowledge comes from God through the fellowship. We are a team and there is a common goal for us. As a group we must stay clear-minded, endure the difficult times so we can be there to spread the Good News of Jesus dying for our sins.

Reflections

Service

Numbers 11:14
"I alone am not able to carry all these people,
because it is too burdensome for me."

Week Forty-Four   **Day Seven**

Moses was at his wit's end. He was fed up with leading God's people. They were never satisfied. They complained constantly. Nothing ever seemed to suit them. They found fault with everything in their daily life. Moses was done!

Ever felt that way? Ever wanted to throw in the towel? Ever just wanted to drive and never come back? I have! Although I never had the kind of responsibility that Moses had, I have been in management all my working career. There is just no way to please everyone. Especially as a Pastor, it seemed like Christians would have been easier to lead, wrong!

The rest of the story with Moses is that God provided seventy elders from among the tribes of Israel. Their job was to take the load off of Moses. They would supplement his leadership within their various tribes. Moses would see the big picture complaints but the other servants would take the lesser load items.

When God asks us to serve it is for that reason. We are needed to help lighten the load for someone else. It's usually not some grand, epic chore. Mostly just giving a brother or sister a break. What a privilege.

Reflections

Worship

Job 2:10
"...Shall we indeed accept good from God and not accept
adversity?"

Week Forty-Five   **Day One**

Boy, oh, boy! This one is a struggle for me. This particular verse is telling us that even when things are going horribly wrong in our lives, we are to accept it as we accept the good. What?! At this point in the story, Job had lost everything – his kids, his home, his everything – except his wife. On top of all that, Job was suffering from boils covering his entire body–painful and not much fun to look at, I'm sure. So, Job's friends and wife are telling him that God only rewards the righteous and does, indeed, punish the sinful. At which point, Job calls his wife "a foolish woman" and tells her that we are to be thankful for the good times and the bad times.

When Charlie went through that hideous trial and was, ultimately found guilty and sentenced to prison, I truly struggled with thankfulness. I had anger and blame and wrath and hurtful thoughts – definitely had that covered. But as time went on and I watched Charlie's faith soar during this time, I realized that 1) God's grace certainly *is* sufficient (2 Corinthians 12:9), and 2) as a result I could trust that all things work together for good. By coming to this realization – being thankful for adversity – my faith and relationship with Jesus has really deepened.

Reflections

Bible Reading

1 Peter 3:15
"Always being ready to make a defense to everyone who asks
you to give an account for the hope that is in you, yet with
gentleness and reverence."

Week Forty-Five   **Day Two**

There is a difference in being a "know-it-all" and knowing your
"stuff." We can be very proficient in our areas of employment
or areas of interests or areas we learn about with our hobbies.
That is much different than being a professed genius in all that
is known by man. Folks who know everything are a bit hard
to take and seldom asked to be around much.

Christians are called to be folks who others want to
be around because they exhibit character traits that are
looked upon as worthy and necessary for a life of peace and
contentment. In 1 Peter 3:15, Peter tells us that we also must,
"…be ready to make a defense to everyone who asks you to give
an account for the hope that is in you…" It goes on to say we
must do it "with gentleness and reverence." We need to know
enough of the Bible so that when people do recognize that we
carry ourselves in a different way than the world, we can give
them an explanation. We may be the only real source of Godly
wisdom they have ever met.

Reflections

Prayer

Psalms 109:21
"But you, O God, the Lord, deal kindly with me for Thy
name's sake; for Your lovingkindness is good, deliver me."

Week Forty-Five **Day Three**

David's not doing well here – he's frail, feeble, and heading for the hills because people are chasing him to kill him. He calls out to God for help and relief. And if it were me, I'd be a-praying for vindication for myself and shame and regret for my enemies. I would, indeed. But, not David. David wants the outcome to show his enemy that his deliverance was directly from the hand of God.

Our prayers, our thoughts, our desires must be like David's. Our hearts and souls and minds must be like Christ's. I long for the day when I more instinctively desire pleasing God and having Him made known to others.

Reflections

Meditation

Luke 24:16
"But their eyes were prevented from recognizing Him."

The very same day Jesus died, was put in the tomb, and rose from the dead, two of His disciples were headed to Emmaus. On their journey, a man, who they did not recognize, joined them. These two, probably Cleopas and his wife, Mary, had just been through a horrific couple of days. I can just hear them recounting all the things that had just happened to their friend Jesus and trying to figure it all out. Most likely they were heartbroken, confused, perhaps hopeless, and probably angry. I can only imagine their conversation was raw and honest as they explained to the stranger what had just transpired to their beloved Jesus.

I suppose meditation is very similar to Cleopas and Mary's verbal explanation of Jesus' arrest, crucifixion, death, burial, and resurrection. Raw, honest, heartfelt. That's what meditation is all about: telling Jesus what happened in our lives and how we are feeling about it. Meditation is a time of revealing it all, no-holds-barred, straight from the heart. It is a time for us to approach God at our most vulnerable and then listen to what He has to say. This last part can be difficult as we may not recognize Jesus in whatever state He comes to us, but also because we haven't trained ourselves to listen. While meditating this week, be especially aware of His words of comfort, forgiveness, loving admonishment, and hope. He will reveal Himself to you!

Reflections

Physical Wellness

Job 19:17
"My breath is offensive to my wife,
and I am loathsome to my own brothers."

Week Forty-Five   **Day Five**

Job, unknowingly, was the focus of a dispute between God and Satan. Satan maintained that Job's faithfulness to God was only because his life was rich in people, things, and power. God maintained that Job's faithfulness was founded on his understanding and faith in God. So, after placing a couple of conditions on Satan, God let Satan have at it with Job. Job lost everything. And I mean everything: his family, his wealth, his health. Even his three friends tried to convince Job that his trials were a direct result of sin in his life. Job refuted this time and time again. He never wavered from his trust in God. And, ultimately, God restored Job's life and health – but in the only way God does things – over the top! He was richer, he was given a new family, and his health was restored.

Please note, dear friends, that poor physical health is not a punishment doled out by God. Just because you may have been born without a limb or you developed MS later in life does not mean God is punishing you. We must recognize that no matter where we find ourselves and what trials we are going through, God will faithfully use us and our situation for His purpose and for His good. Can we all rethink the bad things that happen to us as being opportunities for God? Can we ultimately rejoice in them? Let's try.

Reflections

Fellowship

1 Timothy 3:15
"I write so that you will know how one ought to conduct himself in the household of God, which is the church..."

Week Forty-Five   **Day Six**

I'm sure I've mentioned this a trillion times, but the Bible tells us how to do *everything*! Here, Paul is writing to Timothy and friends, telling them what a healthy church looks like. We don't have to figure it out! It's right there. The church is a body, a family, a collection of sinners; with every group, there are ways one needs to conduct oneself in order for the body, family, church to prosper and give glory to God.

Church is where we learn how to traverse the big, bad world. It is supposed to be a safe place, a sanctuary, if you will, for us to treat one another lovingly, deal with evil and praise God. And we aren't left to figure it out or have someone else make up the rules – God has given us everything.

Reflections

Service

Deuteronomy 21:5b
"...The Lord your God has chosen them to serve Him and to bless in the name of the Lord...."

Week Forty-Five   **Day Seven**

By now, I hope you have come to appreciate the importance of service in the Christian life. In a practical sense, what does that look like? I've always been a big fan of feeding people. I've volunteered at soup kitchens, food drives, and programs that aid at supplementing snacks for the weekend for school aged kids. I also have a heart for women who are struggling; my ability to listen and empathize and mentor young women is another area of service that I really, really enjoy.

I strongly urge all people to volunteer. I raised my kids volunteering and they continue giving of their time and talents today. It's a wonderful thing to do as a couple or family or church group. There are lonely people in nursing homes and rehabs that would love a weekly visit. Working with the homeless is another fantastic area of service. The point is, God chose each of us to serve Him. Go do it!

Reflections

Worship

James 1:5
"But if any of you lack wisdom, let him ask God, who gives to all men generously and without reproach, and it will be given to him."

Week Forty-Six   **Day One**

So, everyone likes getting advice, right? We love when folks proffer their expertise into our life. Usually the stuff that is not asked for brings the most joy, not! Most of us think we are capable. We really do not think we know all the answers. We just do not like getting advice from others. It must just be part of being a human.

James is helping us understand here that trials in life are going to show up. He says, in fact that we need to be pleased when they come. It is just God's way of helping us grow spiritually. That is what this devotional is geared to do, help us get ready for those trials.

James says if you need help in your trials, ask God for wisdom. God wants us to know what the next step is. He is not going to give much more than one step at a time. In His manner, step by step we get through the situation. Developing spiritual disciplines aides in this process as well.

We praise and worship God for this kind of tech support. He is able and wants us to cling to Him during our spiritual journey in this life. He will provide the wisdom we need; we just need to ask.

Reflections

Bible Reading

2 Peter 1:10, 11
"Be all the more diligent to make certain about His calling and choosing you; for as long as you practice these things, you will never stumble, for in this way the entrance into the eternal kingdom of our Lord and Savior Jesus Christ will be abundantly supplied to you."

Week Forty-Six   **Day Two**

Face it, there are things we like about ourselves and there are things we do not like. If we are willing to take an honest look at who we are and our behavior patterns we can get an accurate estimate of our positives and negatives. No big deal, we all have both. It's what we do about them that separates us from some of the lower life forms. If we are willing to make efforts to improve upon the good and shave away the bad then we will be the better for it.

In Peter's second book he tells us that we all have virtues worthy of using to serve God. He says that knowledge, self-control, and perseverance leads to godliness. This godliness leads to brotherly kindness and then to love. In 2 Peter 1:10, he says that we need to "be all the more diligent to make certain about his calling...for as long as you practice these things, you will never stumble." The world cannot offer us this promise, only God's Word. If we seek to find His will for our life and practice these precepts outlined by Peter, we "will never stumble!"

Reflections

Prayer

Proverbs 20:24
"Man's steps are ordained by the Lord; how then can man
understand his way?"

Week Forty-Six   **Day Three**

This verse is so important to understand. God is sovereign
over man's ways. It is hard to comprehend that each one of our
steps is known by God. Every word we say or every thought we
think is known by God. Every action we take in the dark or
light is known by God. All our life - past, present and future -
is known by God.

Our prayer life is so important because He wants us to get
a clue. He wants us to have as much information about what
we need for the next step, thought or word. We actually should
do nothing without checking with God first.

It seems cumbersome, but not actually. We already know
these spiritual disciplines are approved by God. We know
the Golden Rule and about loving our neighbors. We already
practice a lot of God's ways in our life. We need to be getting
information on the other life things. Prayer is our portal. God
wants us to be obedient and He gives us all the tools we need.

Begin to check in with God. King David did always and
was considered a man after God's own heart. That is a pretty
good accolade; it's the one I want.

Reflections

Meditation

Jeremiah 26:13
"Amend your ways and your deeds and obey the voice of the Lord your God; and the Lord will change His mind about the misfortune which He has pronounced against you."

Week Forty-Six   **Day Four**

God is so patient with us. I know growing up my parents were so patient with us kids. At times they looked as us like we were aliens unable to understand earth language. They knew words were coming out of their mouths but we were not moving or giving any indication that obedience was to follow. Thank you, God, for my patient parents.

I too, remember looking at my son in the same way. I know words have been uttered, why are you not responding in kind? Did you not learn from the last event what non-compliance gets you? Thankfully my son was brighter than me and we had a whole lot less "teaching" moments than I did with my parents.

Jeremiah is fighting the same uphill battle we parents often do. Folks will just not listen. Time and time again this faithful prophet tried to lovingly move God's people toward obedience, mostly to no avail. Even when they knew the consequences for their stubbornness, they refused to heed God's warnings. Sounds familiar, right, parents?

Meditate on God's communication with you. Write it down, mull it over, parse the sentences, do whatever. Just spend time in thoughtful exploration on His direction. It saves a lot of heartache and pain, just ask a parent.

Reflections

Physical Wellness

Luke 6:21
"Blessed are you who hunger now, for you shall be satisfied."

Week Forty-Six   **Day Five**

As a member of management, it was always my philosophy to "set the table," for those who I lead. I got in early or stayed late setting out the correct supplies, so those under my leadership would have what they needed to accomplish their mission. There is nothing worse than working for someone who expects you to accomplish a task and yet does not provide the resources to do so.

In our spiritual journey we are to do the best we can with what God provides. He wants us to come to Him for those tools, the things necessary to accomplish His tasks for us. He does not want us going out of the house without our raincoat or rubber boots. He wants us to be prepared.

Dr. Luke is relating events in his gospel what we call in Matthew's gospel the Sermon on the Mount. That discourse is one of the fullest bits of instruction Jesus gave on righteous living. It is a blessing to go to God for our provisions. He wants us to be fit enough to do what He requires and will provide all the tools necessary.

Like all good managers He is setting the table for us. He will never ask from us without providing the resources necessary. It is comforting to know He has our back and has already paved our future.

Reflections

Fellowship

Jonah 1:2
"Arise, go to Nineveh…cry against it, for their wickedness
has come up before Me."

Week Forty-Six   **Day Six**

Have you ever been asked to do something you really do not want to do? The task just seems overwhelming. The people are just not your type so you do not want to help them. The distance is too great, the journey is not worth the effort in your mind. Many other reasons can come to mind where we give ourselves permission to opt out on fellowship opportunities.

Granted, not every human being is someone you wish to expose yourself to. Not every situation is one you wish to participate in. Not every fellowship opportunity is an exciting event designed to give you warm fuzzy feelings.

God is telling Jonah to get out of his comfort zone and preach to the bad folks a long way off. These folks are the enemy and just mean. They are not folks you want to have play dates with. Nevertheless, God told Jonah to go.

It is the same thing He tells us. He has told us not to forsake the fellowship of others. The group is the strength and a source of encouragement. The folks He sends us to be around have a purpose in our spiritual development. Who are we to run and hide? Look where Jonah ended up when he refused to fellowship! Just saying.

Reflections

Service

Matthew 26:10
"Why do you bother the woman? For she has done a good deed for me."

Week Forty-Six   **Day Seven**

At times I still think I am the king of the universe. What I think and say is far superior to those lesser beings around me. I am the center of the universe and all those around me just need to act in accordance with my well-scripted plan for their life. Yep, delusional for sure.

All reality aside, we do often look at what others do and wonder what they have been smoking. How on earth could that be a productive use of their time? What a waste of a perfectly good hour, could you not have found something more productive to do with it?

God tells us to serve each other. God tells us to serve who He wants to bless next. God has a plan for all these actions. Who are we to say they are not appropriate or important? A lady has chosen to use her resources to bless Jesus and got ridiculed for it. Jesus lets all the readers know throughout history that her actions were just right. He knows the future, He has information no one else had. He deems her actions spot on regardless of what the crowd thought. Serve others as God instructs no matter what us geniuses think or say.

Reflections

Worship

1 Peter 1:3
"Blessed be the God and Father...according to His great
mercy has caused us to be born again to a living hope
through the resurrection of Jesus Christ from the dead."

Week Forty-Seven **Day One**

Peter is writing a letter to persecuted Christians in order to comfort them with the truth of eternal life. In his letter he shows us a fitting response to God's mercy: praise! Mercy is when someone withholds a negative consequence which is deserved. And boy oh boy–my God has shown me plenty of mercy. I don't know how many "bullets" I've dodged in my lifetime. Mercy. But God didn't just withhold negative consequences, He gave me eternal life by sacrificing His Son – for my sins – and showed me it is possible by raising Jesus from the dead!!! Grace, on the other hand, is receiving something positive that hasn't been earned or even deserved.

These are things for us to remember when we are worshipping our Lord and Savior. Grace and mercy. Without either, what a horrible, sad life we'd live.

Reflections

Bible Reading

1 John 1:1, 2
"That which was from the beginning, which we have heard,
we have seen with our eyes, which we have looked at and our
hands have touched – this we proclaim concerning the Word
of life. The life appeared; we have seen and bear witness."

Week Forty-Seven   **Day Two**

Our society seems to put very little value on those members who are in their golden years. We stuff them in nursing homes and lock away the history and knowledge they possess. Upon the first glance they seem like fragile, mindless unstable bags of flesh that are waiting for their reward. Yet, if time is taken with them, they are a wealth of knowledge and wisdom. They have made mistakes, learned from them and were able to overcome. They stand as witnesses to what hard work and determination can accomplish.

The disciple John tells us in his first epistle that he and the other disciples of Jesus stand as witnesses to His actions and presence. In 1 John 1:1 he says that "from the beginning, what we have heard, what we have seen with our eyes, what we beheld and our hands handled, concerning the Word of Life." John says he stands as a witness to what happened and that we can count on his accurate retelling of the accounts. We can depend on God's Word as reliable and an accurate way of determining His will for our life. There is no other source of truth and accuracy that we can depend upon.

Reflections

Prayer

Ecclesiastes 7:13
"Consider the work of God, for who is able to straighten
what He has bent?"

Week Forty-Seven   **Day Three**

Today, while I write this, some things in my life have suddenly turned upside down. I'm scared and angry and disappointed and feel very much used. The details don't matter; in fact, think about a situation in your own life in which you had the same feelings and apply them here. Anyway, as I began processing this news and was overwhelmed by it, I quickly realized that the specifics about this circumstance didn't really matter; it is most certainly a spiritual battle for me. My faith is being tested. So, I immediately went to God in prayer. I laid out all my feelings and concerns and down-right fear. I confessed that I was struggling with faith. And I asked for forgiveness for that lack of faith.

There is no doubt in my mind that God can "fix" this little problem of mine. No doubt. And He will. But, through prayer, I have been covered in a blanket of comfort and a knowing that "everything will be okay". I don't know what that looks like but the more time I spend in that sweet place of prayer, the more confident I am that not only will things work out, but that my God will end up making something glorious out of the whole crazy situation.

Reflections

Meditation

Lamentations 1:20a
"See, O Lord, for I am in distress; my spirit is greatly troubled..."

Week Forty-Seven **Day Four**

I tend to run towards God when my butt's on fire and/or "my spirit is greatly troubled" and I'm lamenting. More so than when things are going well. I suppose most of us do. The good news is, although He already knows what's happening in our lives, He wants to hear it from us. I know that I know that I know, without a shadow of a doubt, that my husband loves me. He doesn't have to tell me, but I simply *know* it. However, my little heart leaps every time he tells me (which, by the way, is several times a day!). I need to hear those words. I long to hear those words. But when something is bothering him, I need to hear those words, too. Even if I can't possibly fix the problem, I need to hear him talk about these things; I need the intimacy of shared laments. Sometimes, just having someone listen helps us sort out problems and not feel as if we are carrying that burden alone.

God longs to hear what is on our hearts. He already knows—He wants to hear it from our mouths. Meditation is time in which we can share our greatly troubled spirits with Him AND feel His presence and grace and healing. And often He will use this time to show us a solution or give us comfort. We just need to show up. And tell Him.

Reflections

Physical Wellness

John 15:2
"Every branch in Me that does not bear fruit, He takes away; and every branch that bears fruit, He prunes it so that it may bear more fruit."

Week Forty-Seven   **Day Five**

I've mentioned before that I am crazy about gardening. Watching a plant develop and produce and even struggle is just keenly fascinating to me. Talk about seeing the hand of God.... Anyway, one of the little tasks of gardening is pruning. Pruning is the cutting off of dead stuff – leaves, spent flowers/fruit, branches. This is done to reduce the amount of energy and resources from the useless and dying parts of the plant and allow it to focus on new growth. I began dead-heading (removing spent flowers) a rose bush this year (where previous seasons I didn't). I cannot begin to tell you about the abundance of new growth. Truly astonishing.

In this passage, John is talking about Christians who have been bearing fruit for God and could be of greater assistance and value to Him, but still have some aspects of their lives that prevent them from their full potential. God will "prune" these aspects—and, let me warn you, it is most often painful or at least unpleasant-in order for us to become richer in spiritual growth and of greater service to Him. And, let me warn you again, sometimes the good that results is so good it can be overwhelming – but in a wonderful way! So, the next time you are struggling through something and things simply are not going well, rest in the knowledge that it may just be God getting you ready for His next assignment.

Reflections

Fellowship

Joel 2:11
"The Lord utters His voice before His army,
surely His camp is very great..."

Week Forty-Seven   **Day Six**

"There's strength in numbers". "Alone we can do so little; together we can do so much" (Helen Keller). "Two are better than one" (Ecclesiastes 4:9). Solomon supports this by saying, in the fourth chapter of Ecclesiastes, that if one falls the other is there to pick them up; two people will get warmer together than just one; a single person may be a target for predators, but two people may thwart that thinking. Not only are we told to fellowship with one another, it simply makes sense! How many of us instinctively go to another person when we're facing trouble? Or, for that matter, have good news?

As Christians, fellowship is a time for sharing and support. It is also a time for accountability and praise. It's for strengthening, growing, and coming together under the loving comfort of God. I think it's safe to say that most of us have become a part of some group in which we share interests and goals common to all members. Joining other people who love Jesus and are about abiding by His commandments is extremely powerful. Be a part of this group.

Reflections

Service

Mark 10:45
"For even the Son of Man did not come to be served, but to
serve, and to give His life a ransom for many."

Week Forty-Seven   **Day Seven**

If it was good enough for Christ, shouldn't it be good enough
for us? We say we want to be like Christ, but do we? I think
this Scripture is so powerful in that of all people, Jesus, the
Son of God and Man did not come to be served but came to
earth to serve. Of course, He took it a major step forward and
actually gave His life so that we could have eternal life with
God. We can't even help our neighbor.

Service work is as much a part of being a Christian than
any of these other spiritual disciplines. It's that important.
Jesus modeled that for us: He spent His whole life serving
others. We must let the Holy Spirit develop that desire to serve
in our hearts, so that we may, indeed, be Christ-like!

Reflections

Worship

1 John 2:1, 2
"If anyone sins, we have an Advocate with the Father, Jesus Christ the righteous; and He Himself is the propitiation for our sins; and not for ours only, but also for those of the whole world."

Week Forty-Eight   **Day One**

When I got falsely accused, I was a Pastor, directing a ministry for the homeless and folks with drug and alcohol issues. I had been a Pastor for a bunch of years. I had worked in the community in all sorts of service capacities. I visited folks who were unchurched, did funerals for families I did not even know and reached out to a population that was under-serviced.

So, I get accused of something everyone knew was not ever possible and was amazed that some people did not have my back. The majority were outraged and extremely supportive. There were some that became haters-friends, folks I had tirelessly served, people who had invited me for meals many times. I was astonished and hurt!

John tells us that we have an Advocate! Someone always in our corner, no matter what is going on with us or around us. Some translate this word to mean "helper." A person who comes alongside you to aide in carrying a load. A voice in court, a patron to relate who you really are.

Praise God for His insight in knowing we need an Advocate. When we cannot go any further, our God provides someone to carry us. That is why we worship Him!

Reflections

Bible Reading

Proverbs 18:2
"A fool does not delight in understanding, but only in revealing his own mind."

Week Forty-Eight   **Day Two**

There is a big difference between "humiliation" and "humility." There is an intersecting thought between the two concepts; if you are not humble you will eventually get humiliated. The goal of life is to continue spiritual growth and then use these principles in all areas of our life. The issue we have is getting to the point where we believe we no longer want to learn, be it lazy, some sort of genius complex or lack of real interest in anything. Regardless, if we stop our pursuit of knowledge we stop growing and put ourselves in a bad posture before God.

The wise man who wrote Proverbs 18:2 confirms this ideal when he writes, "A fool does not delight in understanding, but only in revealing his own mind." We cannot be satisfied just pronouncing what we already know or claiming what we believe as the truth. We cannot just proclaim what we think as truth, God's Word says that. The Bible lets us know that only a fool believes he has all the answers. A sure path to humiliation is the continued delusion of supremacy.

Reflections

Prayer

Song of Solomon 2:4
"He has brought me to his banquet hall,
and his banner over me is love."

Week Forty-Eight   **Day Three**

Have you ever been to a funeral and people got up to speak about their friend or relative that had just died? There are poems read, essays orated, tears of appreciation and love flowing. Folks really want those in attendance to know how much they loved that person. Funny stories are told, hidden secrets are revealed about funny quirks the person possessed. I have often just commented to myself I hope I am loved like that.

One of the reasons I believe that people do not pray is that they have no idea how much they are loved by God. He loved us so much He sent His Son to die for our sins. Not the Son's sins, He was sinless, our sins. He provided us a Comforter and Advocate like we talked about earlier in the week. He has secured our place in heaven if we accept His Son as our Savior. That is love.

Solomon invited his wife to a banquet and there was a banner expressing his love. A big banner, like one used to marshal troops during a battle. A big banner able to be seen across the battlefield. He wanted her to know he loves her. This also applies to God's love for us and His church. We pray because God loves us and we want to keep that connection. Unlike the world, when the going gets tough, God will always love us.

Reflections

Meditation

Mark 10:27
"With men it is impossible, but not with God;
for all things are possible with God."

Week Forty-Eight   **Day Four**

Life is not easy. It seems so often that evil is winning the high ground all the time. Good honest people seem to be swept up in the tidal wave of selfishness and greed of the world. The "haves" seem to be always ten steps ahead of the "have nots." No matter how hard you try it seems the honest man, the little guy just cannot get ahead.

In Mark's day as well as ours it just seemed that the privileged folks were the ones blessed by God. They must be, that is why they are privileged. The little guy must be full of sin or else he would be getting ahead and become part of the privileged class.

So, when Jesus tells those listening that it will be hard for a rich man, a privileged man in society to get into heaven, the disciples were astonished. Their first question was, "Who, then can be saved?" It just seemed utter foolishness to the disciples that this known societal norm could not be true. Just because you seem to be blessed with all that you have does not mean that it is coming from God.

Lots of things we believe today and even since Jesus was on earth are not true. Some say suicide is the unpardonable sin, not true. Some say the church is the way to salvation, not true.

We meditate so God can reveal these mysteries to us. He will help us unpack these errors that society has deemed fit to believe. Slowly and methodically our meditation will reveal the truth and we will truly be the privileged ones then.

Reflections

Physical Wellness

2 Chronicles 20:17
"You need not fight in this battle; station yourselves, stand and see the salvation of the Lord on your behalf..."

Week Forty-Eight   **Day Five**

Have you ever had someone come to your rescue? Had a flat tire on the interstate and a good Samaritan stopped and help you change it? Ran out of gas in a sketchy part of town and someone just happened by who had a gas can? Locked your keys in the car in the mall parking lot and a policeman with a jimmy device drove by on patrol? Coincidence, right? Wrong!

There are no small situations in God's economy. Everything about us is important to Him. Every situation in our life is known by God. All circumstances we encounter have teaching significance in our life. God controls our environment and is always there with us.

We prepare for what God has coming up next for us. He prepares us today for our tomorrow. We stay physically well so we can meet the challenges God has for us. We prepare, we labor, we push ourselves to be in the correct posture before God.

Then, after all that, sometimes He says, "Sit back, watch what I can do." He knows we are ready to do battle. He knows we have been diligent in our preparations. Yet, at times He just steps in and allows us to see His work. He wants us to rely on Him and provides us evidence that He can do so.

Reflections

Fellowship

1 Thessalonians 1:8
"The Word of the Lord has sounded forth from you…
also in every place your faith toward God has gone forth,
so that we have no need to say anything."

Week Forty-Eight   **Day Six**

In my travels while I was in the Army, I often came across folks who knew my Dad. Now these folks were General Officers and I was a lowly commissioned officer just starting out. I would get a message that some General wanted to talk to me. Of course, I always wondered what dumb thing I had been caught doing. Inevitably, however, they would want to ask about my Dad. They always had high praise of him. They were a classmate of his at West Point or served with him somewhere. They knew him from time together in Vietnam. No matter how they knew him, they had accolades to heap on him.

I was always honored to have a Dad in such good standing with his peers. I was humbled to know how much work it would take to receive those same kind of tributes. Mostly I was glad to be his son.

Paul is doing that here. He wants the fellowship of believers in Thessalonica to know that he was hearing good things about their fellowship. The word is getting around about how strong their faith is. They were making a name for themselves as this body of believers in this "new way."

A strong vibrant fellowship gets noticed. Being part of one makes this spiritual journey so rewarding. We are meant to plug ourselves into a functioning, faithful group. Is that you?

Reflections

Service

Psalms 100:2
"Serve the Lord with gladness; come before Him with joyful singing."

Week Forty-Eight   **Day Seven**

This brief but beloved psalm calls all men to praise and worship God. It goes on to tell us we must serve Him with gladness. We are to be joyful in our walk with Him. Our role as servants should fill us with a desire to sing for joy.

I once heard that I can be, "humbly grateful or grumbly hateful." I can choose to go through life mad at the world. I can be mad at God. I can be unappreciative of the blessings, mercy and grace I have received, or I can travel happy.

So often I go to visit others and hope they are as uplifted as I am when I leave. I call myself going to encourage them but always I leave lifted up. That is the blessing of service. It always does more for you than the one you served. Yes, they receive a blessing as well. You, however, receive the bigger one.

Understandably we are busy and at times all we can do is take care of ourselves. Nevertheless, time taken to serve others is always rewarding. Time taken to get outside of yourself always proves therapeutic. Never will God put a service opportunity before you that will not be mutually beneficial.

Reflections

Worship

Jude 1:21
"Keep yourselves in love of God, waiting anxiously for the
mercy of our Lord Jesus Christ to eternal life."

Week Forty-Nine   **Day One**

Jude's very brief letter illustrates men at their worst and God at His best. Jude's letter was written to defend against false teachings which were arising in the early churches. In his letter, Jude shows practical ways for Christians to be spiritually resilient against the apostates' attempt to destroy their faith. Jude points out that those who claim to be Christian and yet follow their own desires are the most dangerous kind of non-believers; so, believers must remain strong by focusing on God's love for them, continuing to do His will, and eagerly awaiting Jesus' mercy when He returns.

We Christians must focus on the truth of God's written Word and diligently obey Him. To do that, we must actually know what the Bible tells us. As you worship today, praise and thank God for giving us such exact details to follow.

Reflections

Bible Reading

Psalms 106:12
"Then they believed His words; they sang His praise."

Week Forty-Nine **Day Two**

Growing up there was nothing more comforting than my parents' words of assurance. When life did not treat us kids fair or when we got sick or hurt or scared their words brought great relief and peace. I cannot remember a time ever that my parents did not tell us kids the truth or that they deliberately deceived us for some reason. Even when we had done something wrong, we knew that whatever came next would be fair and they would not lash out at us.

God's people gave Him a fit as He led them to the Promised Land. Even after they arrived, they seemed to wander off at the slightest temptation. God constantly assured them that if they turned from their ways they would again be in the correct posture before Him. In Psalms 106:12, the author writes about the Israelites, "They believed His words, they sang His praise." There is nothing more important for us as Christians than believing the Word of God. He has guarded them through time and made them available to us here and now.

Reflections

Prayer

Jeremiah 1:8
"Do not be afraid of them, For I am with you to deliver you,
declares the Lord."

Week Forty-Nine   **Day Three**

Prayer, I believe, is one of our most powerful tools. Prayer can transport us from being horribly afraid to incredibly peaceful. It is a time of honesty and bearing our souls to the One who loves us like no other. Prayer is our way of "plugging in" to God's power and seeing Him work in others' lives. It is a source of comfort and answers and, to be quite frank, a source of unbelievable awesomeness.

Even Jesus prayed. I figure, if it was important to the Son of God, it certainly must be important for me. Prayer is actually a place I find relief and reassurance. I can't tell you how many times I have been terrified of life, went to God in prayer, and came out full of contentment and filled with a real *knowing* that everything will "be okay". I may not know what that looks like precisely, but I'm good with that. Prayer is the most intimate time to me – a time for coming before my Father, head bowed, on my knees – and being able to throw down me and my messiness to the only One who can do something about it!

Reflections

Meditation

Matthew 25:13
"Be on alert then, for you do not know the day nor the hour."

Week Forty-Nine   **Day Four**

Let's look at the background context of this particular verse. In this parable, ten virgins were invited to a wedding and instructed to bring lamps in order to lead some kind of torch-lit procession. Five of the virgins bring enough oil, five don't. These are called the "foolish virgins." As it turns out, the groom shows up late and the foolish virgins have run out of oil. Of course, they ask the other five to spot them some oil but were denied. They leave to get more oil. Upon their return they find that the procession had already happened and they were not needed and hence, not let back in.

At some point, there will be a point of no return for those who have rejected Christ. The lesson from this parable tells us that we must always be ready for Christ's return. Always. In your meditation time, search your heart. Be alert.

Reflections

Physical Wellness

Romans 8:18
"For I consider the sufferings of this present time are not worthy to be compared with the glory that is to be revealed to us."

Week Forty-Nine   **Day Five**

Paul knew pain. In 2 Corinthians 11:23-29 he talks about hunger, thirst, danger, imprisonment, torture, persecution. He definitely understood physical pain. And yet, he considers all his suffering *not worthy* of the glories that will be revealed one day. That's pretty powerful. Paul promotes the immense and intense glory we have been promised.

This Scripture does not minimize our pain and suffering that we all have suffered to some degree; rather, it gives us another perspective–an eternal one. And it should serve as a reminder that we can trust that God uses every ounce of our pain for His purpose and that purpose is always perfect.

Reflections

Fellowship

Hosea 6:6
"I delight in loyalty rather than sacrifice, and in knowledge
of God rather than burnt offerings."

Week Forty-Nine   **Day Six**

Simple, yet profound. Hosea was a prophet (one of many) who tried to convince the nation of Israel to change its evil ways and return to God in the spirit of faithfulness and honesty. When we come together in the name of Jesus, He isn't interested in legalistic rituals and rote repetitions. I'm not saying that we can't or shouldn't follow a pattern when we fellowship; what I am saying is that God desires we serve Him with devotion, obedience, and love.

Fellowship is a time in which we Christians come to God in a collective nakedness (and folks, please, please note that I am speaking metaphorically here. Do not show up for Wednesday night prayer meeting in your birthday suit!!) before the very One who created us and brought us together! Charlie's son, Brooks, and my kids, Blake and Dane, have become very good friends over the years. It makes my heart so happy when these three men are together enjoying each other. I can't help but think that's what God is looking for in all of us—enjoying one another and collectively worshipping Him.

Reflections

Service

1 Corinthians 1:28
"And the base things of the world and the despised God has chosen, the things that are not, that He might nullify the things that are."

Week Forty-Nine   **Day Seven**

More often than not, God chooses the most unexpected people to carry out His will. These people tend to be simple, hardworking, ordinary folks. He delights in using the weak and the underdog to accomplish grand things – things only He can do. And so it goes with service: God uses us common and average people in order to accomplish what only He can do. He does this so that there is no doubt that God has a hand in whatever is transpiring.

I say often that the Bible is our users' manual. Anything we need to know about being a Christian is laid out in Scripture. And Jesus is our prime example of who to emulate as we walk through our lives. Jesus' life was nothing but service to others. He traveled the last three years of His life doing for others. As I've pointed out before, service work isn't about us showing the ladies in our Sunday School class or our fellow choir members what a good little Christian we are; it is about us having a mind like Christ's. His only motivation in serving others was to demonstrate the power and love of God's will. Let's adopt that very same attitude in our service to others.

Reflections

Worship

Zechariah 1:3
"Thus, says the Lord of hosts, return to Me,
declares the Lord of hosts, that I may return to you,
says the Lord of hosts."

Week Fifty   **Day One**

I work with families who have kids in addiction. It is a tough thing to do because addiction can take control and the families do not know why their child just cannot stop this destructive behavior. I was deep in addiction at one time so I can understand their kids driving force and I attempt to help the families understand.

Time after time families reach out to their kids and ask them to "return to them." The door is open and our arms are opened wide, please return to us. Then a point comes where the doors get closed because of abuse and theft the families suffer at the hands of their addicted kids. It is a sad, painful and exhausting struggle for both the family and the addict.

Here Zechariah is pleading with the people of God to return to Him. This is a call to repentance, not just a plea to return to Jerusalem after the seventy-year captivity in Babylon. God wants us to be His people. He wants to be the God we worship. He will continue to ask, until He does not. At some point in human history Jesus will return and judgment will start. No more asking or pleading, just sentencing.

Reflections

Bible Reading

1 Kings 8:61
"Let your hearts therefore be wholly devoted to the Lord our God, to walk in His statutes and keep His commandments as at this day."

Week Fifty   **Day Two**

When we are kids, we have an idea of what we want out of life. We have plans for our futures and how we are going to spend our time. Most of us, however, do not become what we thought about when we were eight years old. Our interests change, we mature and life has a way of molding us into something other than what we had originally planned. The good news is from the beginning God has had a plan for us and no matter what we thought when we were eight, He has always had a purpose for us.

After King Solomon built the Temple of God in Jerusalem, he dedicated it to God. In his benediction he challenges God's people to stay focused on God's will so they could continue fulfilling the plan He has for them. In 1 Kings 8:61, the author quotes King Solomon, "Let your heart therefore be wholly devoted to the Lord our God, to walk in His statutes and to keep His commandments, as at this day." Devotion to God is the basis of our standing before Him. As we grow and mature in our spirituality, that fact will not change. God has a purpose for our lives, if we are obedient then God's will can be done. It is in that fulfillment of God's purpose where we find peace.

Reflections

Prayer

Matthew 7:11
"If you then, being evil, know how to give good gifts to your children, how much more shall your Father who is in heaven give what is good to those who ask Him!"

Week Fifty   **Day Three**

I have a sister that is a great gift giver. Actually, she is my only sister and co-author of this devotional. Nevertheless, she has always found a way to give unique, tasteful and functional gifts. I guess she just reads folks and hears their wants and then translates that into gifts, whatever. She is a good gift giver.

I, on the other hand am a terrible gift giver. I give functional things like vacuum cleaners, or lawnmowers, stuff folks can use. My son growing up received essentials, stuff he needed, functional life stuff. I am way too practical to waste my money on fluff and glitz.

God, however, is much better at gift giving. In fact, He is the Master. He knows everything and is able to ascertain and fulfill our needs. He is not just practical and functional, He also gives out blessings, mercy and grace. He is a good gift giver.

Our prayers are a big part of what we do or do not receive. We ask in a manner befitting His position and He hears us. He provides according to His will but if we are lined up with Him, we ask and He gives what is good for us.

Reflections

Meditation

Philippians 3:20, 21
"For our citizenship is in heaven, from which we eagerly wait for our Savior…who will transform the body of our humble state into conformity with the body of His glory…"

Week Fifty   **Day Four**

Do you ever think about tomorrow? Think about its possibilities, blessings, challenges, potential or dangers? I'm not trying to play God but just meditating on life in general. Our place in the universe. Our creator. How tomorrow will come in His time with His plan in place.

We are told from an early age, to work hard, stay in school, keep your nose clean, stay away from drugs and alcohol. If you do this, you will be in the correct posture for success. Parents, teachers, Preachers and so on, they too encourage the folks they influence that there is a plan and good will win in the end.

Paul is letting the folks know in the church at Philippi, that something is better coming down the road. He is telling them that what you see now will not always be. We are part of God's kingdom now and we will be made anew someday.

What a wonderful picture to think about. It is so encouraging and motivating for me. I meditate on the promises and allow them to be my new reality for my future. I do not know when but someday this will be my new normal. Think about this for a minute, write below what it means to you.

Reflections

Physical Wellness

Jeremiah 4:4
"Circumcise yourselves to the Lord and remove the foreskins
of your heart…because of the evil of your deeds."

Week Fifty   **Day Five**

Physical wellness is not a mystery. Self-care is the key. In a world where the few support the many, self-care is put on hold. We stay so busy that we do not do what we know will bring us the health we want. Eat right, exercise, get the right amount of sleep and stay away from substances that alter you mind.

Jeremiah is telling us to take our self-care a step further. He says we need to purify our hearts and separate ourselves from the sin of the world. We must remove the stubborn, selfish and self-centered ways of our life. Our evil deeds are a result of allowing these character defects to be in control.

The people of God have been disobedient and now they are getting warned. We are disobedient and this same warning applies to us, as well. We need to get serious about these spiritual disciplines and allow them to move us closer to God.

Again, getting into the correct position before God is not a mystery. We can be obedient one step at a time. Slowly we will be in the shape God wants us to be so we can be useful in His plan for a lost and dying world.

Reflections

Fellowship

Galatians 3:28
"There is neither Jew, nor Greek, there is neither slave nor free man, there is neither male nor female, for you are all one in Christ Jesus."

Week Fifty   **Day Six**

In my book, "Labels," I talk about how God used disenfranchised people - people society casts aside God uses to do great things. My biggest point is that we are more alike than different. I tell a story about pulling my little 1995 red GEO Tracker up next to a brand new red Chevrolet Corvette. I though how different these two vehicles were. Then I began to think about how much they had in common. Tires, horns, steering wheel, wipers, lights and so on. They are actually more the same than different.

Paul is telling the church that we are all the same in Jesus. We are all saved the same way, faith in Jesus. We who are saved will all go to heaven. We are seen by God as saved, not by our sex, color, national heritage, education, or family heritage or anything else.

It is a wonderful thought that God sees us as who we are, His children, and nothing else matters. Jesus will vouch for us in His presence. Satan will try to tell us because of one thing or another we are not worthy. God sees it differently.

We humans, like the red Corvette and the red Tracker, are more alike than different. So, we fellowship with everyone. We do not cull folks out of the group for anything. We look at each other like God looks at us, saved by His grace.

Reflections

Service

Jonah 1:3
"Jonah rose up to flee…from the presence of the Lord. So, he went down to Joppa, found a ship…paid the fare…to go…from the presence of the Lord."

Week Fifty   **Day Seven**

Has God ever asked you to do something you did not want to do? Has He ever asked you to get out of your comfort zone to serve someone else? Has He ever made you uncomfortable with the request He makes during your prayer and meditation time? He has me!

Jonah was asked to go preach to a group of seriously bad folks, dreaded enemies of Jonah's people. Jonah's big issue was that he knew God would allow them to enter into His kingdom if they repented and began to follow Him. That ate up Jonah so he fled from the request.

We all know where that landed him. He was asked a second time and then was obedient. The biggest revival ever happened in Nineveh, and Jonah was a part of that. He finally was obedient and God used him in a powerful way. Jonah was way out of his comfort zone. He never really cherished the idea and was kind of a spoiled sport when Nineveh was spared by God.

Doing what God asks is not an option. He does not socially promote us, give us a pass because we do not want to comply. He keeps asking until we become obedient. It is easier to say yes to God than flee, just ask Jonah.

Reflections

Worship

Malachi 1:4a
"We have been beaten down,
but we will return and build up the ruins..."

Week Fifty-One   **Day One**

Malachi 1:1-5 summarizes the basic spiritual conundrum facing Israel: apathy. Here, Malachi points to the destruction of Edom (and Israel's subsequent sufferings), reminding us that God kept the Israelites despite their struggles. And Israel eventually shows their devotion to God. Worship can be a group thing, but it also can be an individual practice; it can be formal or informal, it can be done "big" or it can be done privately and quietly. Worship is simply acknowledging and honoring our God.

We worship when things are good. We worship when things are bad. The important thing – and one I hope you've picked up on – is that we do it. I'm not even sure if one can really love the Lord and know about the power of the cross and NOT worship. And please don't worry about "doing it right". God knows your heart. Worship Him.

Reflections

Bible Reading

2 Samuel 7:28
"And now, O Lord God, you are God, and your words are
true, and you have promised this good thing to your servant."

Week Fifty-One   **Day Two**

At times as we go through life it seems to us that things just
ought to be better. We feel like we have been obedient to
God, we have developed spiritually and we have done our best
to let those around us see Him through our actions. Yet, we
still seem to have hurdles to jump in the practical day to day
living of our life. There seems to be no difference between the
struggles of non-Christians and ours as Christians. We know
life is not fair but as children of God we feel that He has not
kept His promises.

King David felt much the same way during his life-long
spiritual journey. Time and time again he found himself up
to his neck in opposition and strife. The Psalms he wrote are
filled with cries of anguish and pain. Yet, after being told he
was not going to be the one to build God's temple in Jerusalem,
2 Samuel 7:28 tells us that David, while praying said, "O
Lord, Thou art God, and Thy words are truth, and Thou hast
promised this good thing to Thy servant." David, as should
we, understood that God keeps His promises and even though
to us it looks like He is doing something different, we can
trust Him.

Reflections

Prayer

Matthew 23:14
"Woe to you, scribes and Pharisees, hypocrites, because you devour widows' houses, and for a pretense you make long prayers; therefore, you will receive greater condemnation."

Week Fifty-One   **Day Three**

Have you ever been in church or Bible study or Sunday school class and someone starts praying this long, involved prayer? You know the one: it's so obvious that the one offering the prayer is more interested in entertaining or impressing the listeners. This is a touchy subject—I definitely don't want to judge someone's prayer, but I also feel very strongly that when we pray, we need to take it seriously. Prayer is a very intimate conversation between you and God. He knows what is on our hearts—so, if we are being insincere in our talking with God, He's on to us.

So, this verse is reminding us that, as Christians, we must walk the walk. We don't go to church on Sunday and act all pious, then treat our family, friends, employees badly on Monday, all the while talking about how Christian we are.

Reflections

Meditation

Revelation 7:17
"For the Lamb in the center of the throne will be their shepherd and will guide them to springs of the water of life; and God will wipe every tear from their eyes."

Week Fifty-One   **Day Four**

The seventh chapter of Revelation occurs after the sixth seal is opened. In John's vision, he sees four angels standing at the four corners of Earth and one angel rising with the seal of God. This angel places the seal on the foreheads of 144,000 saved Jews. During the tribulation, these 144,000 are used by God in bringing the unbelievers all over the world the Good News of Jesus. The 144,000 will traverse the horror of the tribulation and have eternal life. During the tribulation, God promises to lead them, to guide them, and even wipe tears from their eyes.

God cares enough to help us through the darkness we all face in life and will gently wipe away our tears. I find that incredibly powerful. And comforting. As I've mentioned earlier, I'm writing this in the middle of 2020 and all its craziness. And hatred. And death. And destruction. I have been in desperate need of comfort, of guidance, of someone wiping my proverbial tears. I find all that when I am diligent in my spiritual walk and relationship with God. I encourage you to meditate on the fact that, even in the worst of times, God has our backs.

Reflections

Physical Wellness

Ephesians 4:16
"From whom the whole body, being fitted and held together by what every joint supplies, according to the proper working of each individual part, causes the growth of the body for building up of itself in love."

Week Fifty-One   **Day Five**

Okay, I'll be honest with you (just don't tell Charlie): I wasn't too crazy when I read *When Life Shows Up* and physical wellness was identified as a spiritual discipline and became even more annoyed at it as I started writing for this devotional. However (you knew that was coming, didn't you?!), I'm a true believer now. During this time of research and prayer, guidance from the Holy Spirit and self-reflection, I understand the importance of my physical body and how I treat it and take care of it.

I still have work to do. I suppose I always will; but my attitude has changed during this time with you about what exactly is housed in this body, and how I care for that house. My whole mindset about loving my physical self, and demonstrating that love through care, has altered and become something that is increasingly important to me. As I said at the beginning of the paragraph, I still have much work to do, many improvements to make. The difference between Week One and today is I truly know that honoring my body IS honoring God.

Reflections

Fellowship

Haggai 2:4
"But now take courage, Zerubbabel,' declares the Lord,
'take courage also, Joshua Son of Jehozadak, the high priest,
and all you people of the land take courage,'
declares the Lord, 'and work; for I am with you,'
declares the Lord of hosts."

Week Fifty-One   **Day Six**

Webster's New Collegiate Dictionary offers three definitions of fellowship: 1) companionship, company, associate; 2) the community of interest, activity, feeling or experience; and 3) partnership, membership. Christian fellowship most certainly can fall in all three categories. You see, the foundation of our relationship with each other is built and molded by our relationship with Christ. As we grow spiritually individually, we begin to understand the importance of coming together, collectively, with a common interest of which Jesus Christ is the core.

True Christian fellowship involves getting together for spiritual purposes. True Christian fellowship is a time for sharing our needs and our praises, for prayer, and for diligently reading, discussing, and following God's Word. We fellowship because God told us to; but, in that fellowship, we are able to encourage one another, share burdens and good stuff in order to offer comfort and hope and love.

Reflections

Service

Daniel 1:12
"Please test your servants for ten days and let us be given
some vegetables to eat and water to drink."

Week Fifty-One   **Day Seven**

I've spent most of this year talking about service work to help unbelievers and people less fortunate and/or simply in need, in order to demonstrate the love of Jesus. Today I want to talk about being of service to fellow believers. I have seen, been a target of, and been a part of behavior and actions between Christians that aren't very, uh, Christian. Dear friends, instead of tearing each other down, ignoring the needs of others, and down-right sabotaging our brothers and sisters in Christ, we – of all people – must come together, knit by the sacrifice of the Cross. If not, how can we know the heart of Jesus Christ? How can anyone know the heart of Christ?

God has provided us with the guidance and directions on how to treat each other. Stop "disguising" gossip as prayer requests; stop rejoicing in another's hard times; do something–anything–for a fellow Christ-lover that is hard for you or, egad, inconvenient for you. Honestly, how are we ever going to spread the Good Word and actually attract unbelievers when our own behavior towards one another is, well, unattractive? Out of the mouth of Jesus Christ, God Himself, the second greatest commandment: "Love your neighbor as yourself" (Matthew 22:39). And, yes, this includes our fellow brothers and sisters.

Reflections

Worship

Revelation 21:23
"And the city has no need of the sun or the moon to shine
upon it, for the glory of God has illumined it,
and its lamp is the Lamb."

Week Fifty-Two   **Day One**

When Moses was leading God's people out of Egypt toward the Promised Land, he had a divine guidance system. We have GPS today; Moses had a pillar of clouds by day and pillar of fire by night. In the description of this magnificent occurrence the best that can be said is the "glory of the Lord shone all about them." What else could it have been?

Don't you know that guidance system was an encouragement to all who viewed it? Everyone was able to see it. No matter how far each individual was away from the center of the camp or the front of the movement column, they could see the glory. There could be no doubt that their pathway was divinely paved for success.

John tells us that this same "glory of God" will illuminate His holy heavenly city. The same glory that has led God's people from the beginning will be there in heaven lighting our way for eternity. Hebrews 13:8 says, "Jesus Christ is the same yesterday, today and tomorrow." I am so glad!

We worship God for that very reason. He will always possess the character we have come to depend upon. Mercy, grace, forgiveness and love will always be the way He relates to us. Regardless of our current standing before Him, these will be His go-to responses. Praise God!

Reflections

Bible Reading

1 Samuel 17:37
"And David said, the Lord who delivered me from the paw of the lion and from the paw of the bear, He will deliver me from the hand of this Philistine."

Week Fifty-Two   **Day Two**

It is hard to find people that we can really depend upon. We have friends and family but even they are not as dependable as we would like. Anyone will give us a ride to work, help us move a couch or install a ceiling fan. Yet, if asked for a kidney, a job recommendation or a mortgage payment, they are nowhere to be found. We can count on some people sometimes and some people never, it becomes clear to us.

Young shepherd David understood this concept. When he was talking to King Saul about taking on the giant Goliath, he knew God would protect him. In 1 Samuel 17:37, David tells King Saul, "The Lord who delivered me from the paw of the lion and from the paw of the bear, He will deliver me from the hand of this Philistine." Because of David's past experience with God, he knows that God is dependable and will always be there for him. God's Word is important to us because even if we believe God has failed us, we can look at true evidence and see that He has never failed His children.

Reflections

Prayer

Psalms 5:1, 2
"Give ear to my words, O Lord, consider my groaning.
Heed the sound of my cry for help, my King and my God,
for to Thee do I pray."

Week Fifty-Two   **Day Three**

One of the most frustrating times of my life was when I was on trial for something I did not do. I had spent three years in and out of court rooms leading up to the trial. I had consistently proclaimed my innocence and there was absolutely nothing that would prove it differently. When you have not done something there is nothing there to say you did.

There was only one voice saying I had committed a crime. Of all the voices saying I was honest, wholesome and upright, there was only one dissenting voice. Finally, the trial was started and there was only one prosecuting witness, this lone voice. All the other voices on the stand that day were uplifting and vouched for my character, ministry and service to the community. Nevertheless, the one small voice took the day and I spent the next five years in prison.

I know what David is talking about when he asks God to give "ear" to his words, hear his "groaning," to hear his "cry." To not be heard is a hopeless feeling. For those around you to not understand the depth of your loneliness, to be swallowed up by life and its injustices is too much to bear at times.

God hears our prayers. He knows our circumstances. He is well aware of where we are and who is swarming around us. God will allow us to go through tough times but His promise is that we will never go it alone. Prayer is the way to keep gaining traction in the slippery times of life.

Reflections

Meditation

Titus 2:11, 12
"For the grace of God has appeared, bringing salvation to all men, instructing us to deny ungodliness and worldly desires and to live sensibly, righteously and godly in the present age…"

Week Fifty-Two   **Day Four**

My grandparents were all born in the early 1900's. My parents were both born in the mid 1930's. I was born in 1959. My grandmother was nearly crippled when a wagon pulled by horse ran over her feet. She would later in life drive a car and fly on an airplane. My Dad used a slide rule to do his engineering calculations while a cadet at West Point. He would later work at the Pentagon in a room that housed a bulky computer system. I went to The Citadel with an expensive Texas Instrument calculator, with all the math functions on it. Today I have a cell phone that can do all those calculations or ask Google to do them for me.

The times sure have changed. The world seems to be busier and personal communication seems to be a dying art. I am a fan of technology and advancement. I am also a fan of simplicity and peace. These ideas seem to be diametrically opposed to each other.

With all that is going on in our ever-evolving world, Paul's truth he gives to his friend Titus is still the same. It rang true back then and is still pertinent today. We need to continually meditate on this very truth. It is the cornerstone of our spiritual movement forward. God's grace has given us the opportunity to get in the right posture before Him. To stay there we must deny the lie Satan offers through the world.

Reflections

Physical Wellness

Micah 7:9
"I will bear the indignation of the Lord because I have sinned against Him, until He pleads my case and executes justice for me."

Week Fifty-Two   **Day Five**

This is the last week of the year. By now it is my prayer that you have begun to see the importance of physical wellness as a real spiritual discipline. It is rarely ever talked about and yet a key to our spiritual growth. God will use someone else if we are not properly prepared. If we miss the blessings of God, a chain reaction may start, then we cannot see our way to move forward and we get lazy or even apostate.

Micah is talking to the folks in Jerusalem. He is bemoaning their sinfulness. It is universal, unrestrained, involves the leaders and exhibits itself in perverse and unnatural ways. It's everywhere and has become a problem for folks trying to be right before God.

Apostasy is the slow movement away from God. It is the gradual events of disobedience that moves you off the path traveled by God's people. Suddenly you wake up and you find yourself so off course.

Self-care, in the form of physical wellness, is a perfect place for apostasy to creep into your spiritual journey. You put off diet, exercise and sleep. Soon you are not praying, meditating or worshipping with other believers. You stop serving others and reading your Bible. There is no real reason why, just lifestyle choices that seem little but ultimately move you away from God. Make a promise to check yourself regularly in this area in the upcoming year.

Reflections

Fellowship

1 John 3:16
"We know love by this, that He laid down His life for us;
and we ought to lay down our lives for the brethren."

Week Fifty-Two   **Day Six**

In John's gospel he tells us that Jesus said, "All men will know you are My disciples if you have love for one another" (John 13:35). That is so true. The world tells us that selfishness and self-centeredness is the key to survival. You are number one, look out for yourself. You do not need anyone to be a success in life.

Wow, what kind of crazy is that? All year we have seen that God's plan is in the fellowship of believers where the power and strength of God gets focused. We need each other's strengths to make the execution of God's plan possible.

In this later letter by John he takes our fellowship responsibilities one step further. Jesus laid down His life for us so we should be willing to do so for the fellowship. That is the way to truly show love. In context, the world of that day was more than willing to give Christians the opportunity to lay down their lives for each other.

Isn't it the same way today? Satan wants us dead and is willing to throw us all under the bus before God. He has an army of lost folks to help him place us all in tedious, life threatening positions. Without each other willing to get each other's back Satan would win.

We know the rest of the story. God's plan, His way of showing love ultimately wins the day. We need to never forsake the fellowship, stay attuned to each other's needs and give as much as we get.

Reflections

Service

Amos 8:7
"The Lord has sworn…
I will never forget any of their deeds."

Week Fifty-Two   **Day Seven**

It seems sometimes that the evil of the world is winning. The deeds of the lost seem to profit them more than the deeds we as God's people perform. Living by God's rules seems to accomplish little while the world's ways are profitable.

Amos was just a simple sheep breeder. He was a layman called into service by God. Not seminary trained or a professional orator, just a guy willing to serve as called. A guy who experienced the same frustrations with an evil world of the day as we do today.

His words today are meant to encourage those of the day he was talking to. He is telling them that God will not forget the evil deeds of those around His people. Later he goes on to describe the things these folks will have to endure as a result of their deeds.

We are to be obedient no matter what the circumstances look like. We know through God's Word that God sees all that is going on around us. Our call is to serve as God instructs no matter how frustrating the world makes us. We will be the ones rewarded when we stand before Him in heaven.

Reflections